CONTENTS

Morristown Centennial Library
Regulations
(802) 888-3853
www.centenniallibrary.org
centenniallib2@yahoo.com

Unless a shorter time is indicated, books and magazines may be borrowed for four weeks, audio books on tape and CD may be borrowed for three weeks, and videos and DVDs may be borrowed for one week. All library materials may be renewed once for the same time period.

A fine of five cents a day every day open will be charged on all overdue library books and audio books. A fine of one dollar a day every day open will be charged for overdue library videos and DVDs.

No library material is to be lent out of the household of the borrower.

All damage to library materials beyond reasonable wear and all losses shall be made good by the borrower.

Library Hours

Sunday & Monday	Closed
Tuesday	9:30am – 7 pm
Wednesday	9:30am – 7pm
Thursday	10am – 5:30pm
Friday	10am – 5:30pm
Saturday	9am – 2pm

CULTURES OF THE WORLD
Brazil

Marshall Cavendish
Benchmark
New York

PRECEDING PAGE
Accessible only by sea or hiking trail, the Praia do Sancho on the Archipelago Fernando de Noronha is teeming with a wide variety of marine wildlife and is one of Brazil's most popular beaches.

Publisher (U.S.): Michelle Bisson
Writers: Christopher Richard, Leslie Jermyn and Michael Spilling
Editors: Deborah Grahame-Smith, Mindy Pang
Copyreader: Sherry Chiger
Designers: Nancy Sabato, Benson Tan
Cover picture researcher: Tracey Engel
Picture researcher: Joshua Ang

Marshall Cavendish Benchmark
99 White Plains Road
Tarrytown, NY 10591
Website: www.marshallcavendish.us

Library of Congress Cataloging-in-Publication Data
Richard, Christopher, 1959-
  Brazil / Christopher Richard, Leslie Jermyn, and Michael Spilling. — 3rd ed.
    p.cm. — (Cultures of the world)
  Includes bibliographical references and index.
  Summary: "Provides comprehensive information on the geography, history, wildlife, governmental structure, economy, cultural diversity, peoples, religion, and culture of Brazil"—Provided by publisher.
  ISBN 978-1-60870-798-0 (print) — ISBN 978-1-60870-806-2 (ebook)
  1. Brazil—Juvenile literature. I. Jermyn, Leslie. II. Spilling, Michael.
III. Title. IV. Series.

F2508.5.R53 2012
981—dc23   2011023036

Printed in Malaysia
7 6 5 4 3 2 1

BRAZIL TODAY

BRAZIL INSPIRES DIFFERENT IMAGES FOR DIFFERENT PEOPLE. Some see one big tropical rain forest filled with curious creatures and raging rivers. Others picture the brilliant sights and sounds of Carnival in Rio. Still others imagine miles of pristine beaches. For many, Brazil conjures images of a beautiful and friendly people as diverse as the land they inhabit.

Brazil encompasses all this and more. It's the country where you'll find the greatest number of bird and mammal species in the world. It's the home of some of the world's greatest soccer players and the only country to have won the FIFA World Cup five times. It's where African and European cultures and religions blend in harmony. It's the home of a dazzling array of music and dance styles and some of the most remarkable artists in the Western Hemisphere.

Brazil has much to offer tourists and visitors with its breathtaking nature combined with its exciting cities. However, Brazil also has to overcome some difficult issues, such as poverty and threats to its natural environment. Despite these problems, Brazil has much to celebrate.

One such celebration took place on January 1, 2011—a momentous day for Brazil—as Dilma Vana Rousseff was appointed the 36th president of Brazil. She is

Giant lily leaves dot the swampy landscape of the Amazonian forest in Manaus.

not only the first woman to hold the office in the country, but in 2005 she became the first woman to serve as Brazil's chief of staff. In a country where traditional macho attitudes prevail both at home and at work, the achievements of Dilma Rousseff are considerable. More than 30,000 people gathered to celebrate her historic inauguration. Although Rousseff is leading Brazil at a time when the country is enjoying an unprecedented economic boom and impressive economic growth rates, she has made clear that there is much more to be done to make Brazilian society an equal and fair country. In her inaugural speech, Rousseff pledged to continue the work of her popular predecessor Luiz Inácio Lula da Silva (2003—11), known as President Lula, to eradicate poverty and hunger among the poor and protect the most vulnerable in society. Of course, many antipoverty programs, such as Bolsa Família, which began in 1995 to provide financial aid to poor families on condition that their children attended school and were vaccinated, were established before Lula came into power.

In the past, Brazil's economy followed the pattern of "boom and bust." High inflation and a crippling foreign debt significantly hindered its economic growth. Brazil was helped by economic aid packages offered by the International Monetary Fund (IMF) several times in its recent history. However, building on the legacy of his predecessor President Fernando Henrique Cardoso (1995—2003), President Lula introduced a series of privatizations and strict reforms throughout the 2000s that stabilized its economy and reduced its debt substantially.

As with many other countries around the world, Brazil's economy suffered a slowdown due to the global financial crisis of 2008. It recovered well, however, and has since performed strongly. The government plans to boost consumer demand by increasing the national minimum monthly wage and to limit inflation and control the inflow of capital.

Brazil's robust economy has continued to outperform the economies of more-developed countries. Brazil has particularly been helped in recent years by its strategic economic relationship with China, another emerging economic powerhouse. In 2009 China became Brazil's biggest trading partner, displacing the United States for the first time. Brazil's main exports to China, including soya, grain, oil, and iron ore, account for more than 12 percent of its total exports. It has been calculated that between 2000 and 2009 Brazil's exports to China increased by more than 88 percent. Although Brazil has clearly benefited from its exports to China in recent times, the relationship is also competitive, and imports from China are outselling some domestic products in Brazil. Some Brazilian economists and businesses fear that as Brazil's currency strengthens, it will eventually suffer as Chinese exports become cheaper in comparison.

Despite its spectacular economic growth in the 2000s, Brazil remains an unequal society with millions of people living below the poverty line. The wide gap between rich and poor is most evident in the big cities of Rio de Janeiro and São Paulo, where the rich live in luxurious homes alongside the very poor, who make up 20 to 30 percent of the population and live in slum areas called favelas.

The Brazilian government has been more effective than some other governments in trying to help the impoverished and more-vulnerable people in their society. For example, Brazil's National AIDS Program (NAP) in partnership with civil society groups has become an exemplary model for other developing countries. By battling against the powerful pharmaceutical companies to produce its own more affordable drugs to fight acquired immune deficiency syndrome (AIDS), Brazil has managed against the odds to stabilize the rate of human immunodeficiency virus (HIV) infection and decrease the number of AIDS-related deaths. Another way the Brazilian government has helped its poor is by its active support of the redistribution of land previously owned by a tiny wealthy minority. To draw attention to this particular type of inequality, the Landless Workers' Movement, formed in 1984 by rural workers, has organized many protests and land occupations, demanding the redistribution of arable land from the rich to the poor.

Apart from the complex challenges involved in eliminating poverty, Brazil also faces environmental problems caused by, among other things, droughts and illegal logging. In the past decade, Brazil has suffered from severe droughts, most notably in 2005 and 2010. Scientists believe that the drought of 2010 was more threatening than that of 2005, destroying millions of precious trees in the rain forest. This concerns environmentalists, as it severely curtails the Amazonian rain forests' capability to absorb carbon dioxide, a key factor in preventing the negative effects of global warming. According to measurements taken in Brazil during drought periods, the amount of carbon dioxide released has in fact been higher than the amount being absorbed.

Besides the destruction of millions of trees, the drought in 2010 also caused the Amazon River and many of its tributaries to dry to their lowest levels since 1963, resulting in a state of emergency being declared in more than 25 municipalities within the Amazon Basin. To help the worst-hit regions, the Brazilian government committed $13.5 million in emergency aid specifically to ensure availability of drinking water and food delivery to those people living in the affected areas. The drought also hurt the fishing industry, resulting in many job losses in the region. Another environmental problem is the continued deforestation of the Amazon by loggers and cattle ranchers. In 2005 it was estimated that 20 percent of the rain forests had been cleared by deforestation. In spite of the government's efforts to mitigate illegal logging and establish improved certification of land ownership, reports indicate that the governmental reforms have not brought about much-needed change, and the situation has not improved. Brazil will host the Rio Plus 20 global environmental summit in 2012, where many of these issues will be debated.

Critics are accusing the Brazilian government of adding to these existing problems by constructing the world's third-biggest hydroelectric dam, the 3.75-mile-long (6-km-long) Belo Monte Dam, on the Xingu River, a tributary of the Amazon in the northern state of Pará. Although the government believes that this development will bring vital jobs to the region, many others believe that this massive construction project will instead destroy the already fragile ecosystem and render at least 50,000 indigenous people homeless. To appease the protestors both in Brazil and around the world, the government has promised to seriously consider environmental and social issues that will emerge from this huge development.

Brazil is blessed with a plethora of rich mineral deposits, including iron, petroleum, bauxite, coal, and manganese. As these are in great demand and highly valued by major manufacturing countries such as China, Brazil can be confident of its economic prospects. Another of Brazil's recent achievements is that it has managed to become self-sufficient in crude oil, due to the development of its own offshore fields. This means that some areas of Brazil, unlike many other countries, will no longer have to rely on foreign supplies of crude oil.

Growth in Brazil is stimulated by the nation's preparations to host two prestigious international sporting events: the 2014 FIFA World Cup and the 2016 Summer Olympics.

Portions of the Amazonian rain forest are being destroyed by various mining, industrial, and construction works carried out in Brazil.

Brazil will become the fifth country to have hosted the FIFA World Cup twice. Twelve cities have been chosen to host the soccer matches, including São Paulo, Rio de Janeiro, Belo Horizonte, Porto Alegre, Brasília, Cuiabá, Curitiba, Fortaleza, Manaus, Natal, Recife, and Salvador. The venue for the anticipated final match will be the famous Maracanã Stadium in Rio de Janeiro. Billions will be spent on modernizing the infrastructure of Brazil. An estimated $1 billion will be spent on upgrading and building stadiums. A further $6.25 billion will be invested in constructing a high-speed rail system connecting the cities of Campinas, São Paulo, and Rio de Janeiro.

The Rio de Janeiro 2016 Summer Olympic Games will be the first games held in South America. The Olympic Village will be built in the district of Barra da Tijuca. The other three venues will be Copacabana Beach, Maracanã Stadium, and Deodoro. However, the International Olympic Committee has expressed concern over security issues in Rio de Janeiro. The preparations for the Games will include a strong focus among the people of Rio and the governing bodies on reducing the high levels of crime in the city.

Brazil assumed a nonpermanent seat on the United Nations Security Council for the 2010-2011 term, and it is seeking a permanent seat. As an economic powerhouse and one of the world's biggest democracies, Brazil is and will most likely continue to be South America's most influential country and a leading global nation.

GEOGRAPHY

Located in the Fernando de Noronha National Marine Sanctuary in the state of Pernambuco, the Baía dos Porcos (Pigs' Bay) beach is famous for Dos Hermanos, the two rocks jutting out of the ocean (*at top of picture*).

1

BRAZIL IS THE LARGEST COUNTRY in South America, taking up almost half of the land area of the continent, with an area of 3,286,502 square miles (8,512,001 square km). Brazil is as large as the whole of Europe and is so vast that it borders every South American country except Chile and Ecuador. It has the world's longest continuous coastline, with 4,655 miles (7,491 km).

Brazil is the fifth-largest country in the world. It's also the sixth most populous nation, after China, India, the United States, Indonesia, and the Russian Federation.

The stark sand dune fields in Lençóis Maranhenses National Park in Maranhão.

An aerial view of the Amazon lakes of the Madeirinha River in Brazil.

Brazil's easternmost piece of land is closer to Africa than to its southern border with Uruguay. A traveler on a ship several miles up the Amazon River would have a hard time distinguishing the river from the ocean. Although the width of the Amazon varies from about a mile (1.6 km) to 30 miles (48 km) depending on the season, the mouth of the river, where it enters the Atlantic Ocean, measures about 200 miles (322 km) wide.

The equator runs across the north of Brazil, and 90 percent of the country lies in the tropical zone. The remaining 10 percent, in the south, is in the temperate zone. More than half of Brazil lies 2,000 feet (609 m) or more above sea level. While the Amazon Basin is covered in tropical rain forest, the central area is mainly savanna with sparse vegetation. One-fourth of all known plant species and a third of all iron-ore reserves are found in Brazil.

The country can be divided into five regions: The north and the central west have few people but great economic potential, the northeast is rich in history but poor in wealth, and the southeast and the south are home to most of the population and wealth.

THE AMAZON

The largest part of the Amazon rain forest is located in Brazil, covering more than 60 percent of the country. It spans the borders of eight countries and is the world's largest river basin and the source of one-fifth of all free-flowing freshwater on earth. The Amazon rain forest receives more than 80 inches (2,032 mm) of rain a year in some areas. The vast Amazon is the world's largest river basin and tropical rain forest. Scientists believe that the Amazon River and jungle produce one-third of the world's oxygen and hold one-fifth of its freshwater resources.

MIRACLE PLANTS

The first explorers who crossed the Andes Mountains found Indians using a white crystal extracted from the bark of the cinchona tree as medicine (below). Hundreds of years later, scientists discovered that this crystal, called quinine, effectively protects people from the tropical disease malaria.

Today scientists known as ethnobotanists believe that plants in the Amazon might hold a cure for many diseases and that the disappearing rain forests and the indigenous people who live in them should be protected.

Ethnobotanists depend on the Indians' knowledge of the jungle just as much as they depend on chemistry or biology. Scientists are now exploring the jungle with indigenous medicine men and observing the way they put plants to use: how a liquid squeezed from a fungus growing on dead trees can be used to treat earaches or tea made from a red berry can be used to fight fevers. With the richness of the Amazon's biodiversity, perhaps one day ethnobotanists will discover more medicinal cures for some of the world's most serious illnesses.

The Amazon River is fed by more than 1,000 tributaries, 17 of which are more than 1,000 miles (1,609 km) long. It is the second longest river in the world, running 4,000 miles (6,437 km) from where it starts in the Andes Mountains to where it drains into the Atlantic Ocean. Every second, it sends an average of 7.4 million gallons (209 million l) of water into the Atlantic Ocean—more than the output of the next three biggest rivers in the world put together. The Amazon receives water from the Andes Mountains in the west, the Guyana Highlands in the north, and Brazil's Central Plateau in the south. The river drains an area almost the size of Australia.

The Amazonian jungle, which covers most of this basin, makes up one-third of the world's natural forests. Over the years, its mystery has attracted countless explorers. The Spaniards searched it for the mythical El Dorado, a city made of gold, 400 years ago. The Spaniards also created another myth, that of a fierce group of women warriors called Amazons, which gave the area its name. Today explorers in the Amazon still find Indians who have never met an outsider, and scientists there still discover new kinds of insects and animals. Botanists believe that the 25,000 plants cataloged represent only half of the jungle's total plant population. Containing nearly 40,000 species of plants, including trees, flowers, herbs, bushes, grasses, vines, ferns, and mosses, the Amazon sustains the world's richest diversity of freshwater fish, birds, and butterflies. Many trees reach 200 feet (61 m) in height, forming a continuous canopy, blocking out almost all sunlight from the forest floor. Rivers crisscross the area, and tropical storms frequently cause flooding.

Countless strange creatures exist among the Amazon's 10,000 known species, such as howler monkeys, whose screams can be heard miles away, and ant armies that devour plants and animals in their path.

A mother and her children rowing a canoe along the Amazon River. Besides sustaining wildlife, the rain forest also supports the lifestyles of many Indian communities.

THE CENTRAL WEST

The central west contains four states and the Federal District of Brasília. With about 3.789 million residents (2009), the Federal District has a population larger than three of the region's four states. The government built Brasília from scratch and made it the nation's capital in 1960, hoping that this would spur the region's development. However, the plan did not initially work out well. While Brasília grew, the rest of the region did not. In the 1970s, though, the central west boomed. About 100,000 people moved in each year, making it Brazil's "Wild West." Landowners still hire gunmen, or *pistoleiros* (piss-toh-LEH-rohs), to keep squatters off their property, and guns often replace the law in frontier towns.

Almost the entire region sits on the Central Plateau, a huge plain 3,353 feet (1,022 m) above sea level. Scrub brush and small trees cover most of the land, but rich red soil lies underneath. The region has already become a major cattle-raising area, and increasing amounts of land are being cultivated. Many people fear that settlers pouring into the region will cause serious damage to the environment, and this may alter the ecology of the entire world. Farmers use the slash-and-burn technique to prepare new fields: They cut down the vegetation and then burn it. Satellites have detected heat from thousands of small fires in the region, and scientists fear that this is contributing to the warming of the planet.

Brasília, the nation's capital, captured the world's imagination during its construction in the 1950s.

The cobbled streets and architecture in Largo do Pelourinho in Salvador da Bahia show a blend of European and Brazilian styles in their pastel-colored façades. Declared a **UNESCO** World Heritage Site in 1985, this **Centro Historico** (Historical Center) is now an important cultural center and major tourist attraction.

Economic development also threatens the Gran Pantanal, a low swampland off the Central Plateau along the Paraguay River. Pollution from mining and the growth of cattle herds endanger the fragile balance of this wildlife preserve along the border with Bolivia and Paraguay.

Rains flood the Gran Pantanal between October and March. More than 350 types of fish thrive on the plants in the swollen rivers and spawn during this period. Then comes the dry season, when water levels fall, trapping fish in landlocked lakes. These fish make easy prey for the 600 species of birds that nest in the Gran Pantanal. Alligators also feed on these fish and are hunted for their skins, which fetch a good price on the international market.

Yet humans are not the ultimate predators in the Gran Pantanal. When piranhas are trapped in lakes in the dry season, their normal diet of small fish runs out, and they turn to larger animals and even people for food.

THE NORTHEAST

Nine states along the Atlantic coast make up the northeastern region, approximately 18 percent of Brazil's territory. This was the first area to be colonized by the Portuguese 500 years ago. The major coastal cities of Recife, Maceió, and Salvador have beautiful beaches and areas of historical interest.

UNESCO made Pelourinho in Salvador da Bahia a World Heritage Site in 1985. The northeast is also the least developed part of the country, with little industry and poor agriculture.

Severe drought regularly plagues the northeastern region. Terrible droughts came between 1877 and 1919, causing 2 million deaths, and Brazil continues to suffer from severe droughts. The most recent disasters of 2005 and 2010 caused the declaration of a state of emergency in more than 20 municipalities.

A narrow, fertile strip follows the coastline from the city of Natal south through the state of Bahia. Here, cocoa and sugarcane plantations thrive if there is enough rain. A line of white sandy beaches along the coast makes this a popular area for tourists. Beyond the majestic beaches lies the immense dry backland known as the *sertão* (seh-TAUN). Only cacti and scrub brush break up the dusty brown earth in this zone. Rain never falls during the first six months of the year; then it comes in sudden storms. A few hours will produce most of the rainfall for an entire year, and flash floods can be a problem. Life is very difficult for the inhabitants of this region, who try to squeeze out a living by raising cattle.

One major river, the São Francisco, breaks up the dry scenery of the *sertão*. It serves as a source of water and energy and as a means of transportation for the region. Barges and ferries patrol the 1,800-mile (2,897-km) river, including a U.S. steamboat built in 1913 for use on the Mississippi River. The river's water enables some farming to take place along its banks. The Paulo Afonso dam and power plant in Bahia also generates electricity for much of the region.

A farmer's hut on the roadside in the dry northeastern hinterland of Bahia. The interior of this region, called the *sertão*, is devastated by severe drought and poverty.

THE SOUTHEAST

The iconic *Christ the Redeemer* statue on Corcovado Mountain overlooks the Cidade Maravilhosa or "Marvelous City," of Rio de Janeiro. Apart from being a symbol of Christianity, the statue's open arms are seen by many as a testament to the warmth of the Brazilian people.

THE SOUTHEAST

The southeast is the most developed, industrialized, and populated region. Made up of the states of Minas Gerais, Espírito Santo, Rio de Janeiro, and São Paulo, the southeast accounts for only 11 percent of the nation's land but contains the three largest cities—São Paulo, Rio de Janeiro, and Belo Horizonte—and a third of the national population. The region's moderate climate makes it an important agricultural area and has encouraged settlement and the growth of multiple industries.

São Paulo is the business capital of Brazil, accounting for a third of the nation's industrial output. One of the largest cities in the world, São Paulo has a metropolitan population of about 20 million people, many of whom come from other parts of the world. Millions of Brazilians have also poured into the city from the northeast.

Brazilians fondly call Rio de Janeiro, a city of about 12 million residents, the Cidade Maravilhosa, or Marvelous City. Pão de Açúcar, or Sugar Loaf Mountain, is a bare granite rock guarding the entrance to the Guanabara Bay. A string of beautiful beaches, starting with Copacabana and Ipanema, line the coast. In spite of having lost its roles as the leading business center and the nation's capital, Rio remains Brazil's top tourist destination.

Belo Horizonte is the capital of Minas Gerais. Located on a plateau about 2,500 feet (762 m) above sea level, Minas Gerais has been an important mining center for 300 years. Three-quarters of the world's gold found in the 18th century came from Minas Gerais. Today it is a major source of iron ore and valuable gems.

Most of the state of São Paulo sits on this same plateau. Here, the red soil and temperate climate are perfect for growing coffee, and this financed the growth of São Paulo. Today Brazil is by far the world's top exporter of coffee.

THE SOUTH

The smallest of the five regions, the south is a cattle and agricultural center. Its three states all fall below the Tropic of Capricorn. The temperate climate has attracted European immigrants from Italy and Germany.

A low mountain range dominates the region, starting in the center of the state of Rio Grande do Sul and ending at the Central Plateau. Rio Grande do Sul is one of Brazil's richest states and is known as the breadbasket of the south. The state is Brazil's largest rice producer, second-largest wheat producer, and third-largest corn and soybean producer. The south of Rio Grande do Sul is a flat grassland, an extension of the pampas of Argentina. This is still Brazil's main cattle-raising area. Residents here are called gauchos, after the cowboys who round up the herds on the pampas.

The Paraná River dominates Brazil's third major river system. It joins the Paraguay River in Argentina before emptying into the Atlantic Ocean. At the point where Brazil meets Argentina and Paraguay lie the Iguaçú Falls, which are the result of a volcanic eruption. This area consists of 275 independent falls spread over 2.67 miles (4.29 km), producing a roar that can be heard several miles away. The most spectacular view is at Devil's Throat, where 14 falls drop 350 feet (107 m) with such force that there is always a 100-feet (30-m) cloud of spray overhead.

Itaipu Dam, the heart of the world's largest hydroelectric plant, is located on the Paraná River along the border with Paraguay, a few miles from Iguaçú Falls. It is a complex of five dams stretching 5 miles (8 km). The main dam soars

The Itaipu Dam, located between Brazil and Paraguay on the Paraná River, is one of the largest operating hydroelectric facilities in the world.

as high as a 65-story building, with its magnificent powerhouse measuring one-half mile (approximately a kilometer) long. The dam's reservoir is also Brazil's largest lake. Built from 1975 to 1991, it is a binational undertaking run by Brazil and Paraguay. The total production capacity of the power plant's 20 units generates 14,000 milliwatts of hydroelectricity, 78 percent of which goes to Paraguay and 22 percent to Brazil.

CLIMATE

Brazil, influenced by its transcontinental geographical configuration, possesses a broad climatic diversification. It has five climatic regions: equatorial, tropical, semiarid, coastal, and subtropical. Therefore, temperatures and rainfall vary for different parts of the country.

Because Brazil embraces a great part of the Amazon Basin in the north, the climate there is humid with heavy rainfall year-round. Influenced by the marine tropical mass, the coastal area is hot and humid, with slightly less rainfall. In the central regions, it is semihumid—hot and wet in the summer and drier and cooler in the winter. In the south, it is humid with regular rainfall and occasional snowfall and frost.

The temperature varies from an average of 52° F (11°C) in June to an average of 86°F (30°C) in September. The average temperature in Brazil is 71°F (21.5°C). Brazil receives an average of 55.7 inches (141 mm) of rainfall per year. The average annual relative humidity is 68.3 percent.

INTERNET LINKS

http://nationalzoo.si.edu/Animals/Amazonia/Facts/basinfacts.cfm

This website of the Smithsonian National Zoological Park provides useful information, facts, and figures about the Amazon Basin.

www.mapsofworld.com/brazil/information/climate.html

This website provides a comprehensive account of the varying climates in different regions of Brazil, including facts about temperature and rainfall levels.

http://countrystudies.us/brazil/20.htm

This website provides general information about Brazil's geography, covering topics such as its geology, geomorphology, drainage, soils and vegetation, climate, and geographic regions.

www.ibge.gov.br/english/

The Brazilian Institute of Geography and Statistics (Instituto Brasileiro de Geografia e Estatística, or IBGE) provides online access to information and data about the country's geography and population status.

www.brazilink.org/tiki-index.php

This website provides useful links to government websites, academic sources, nongovernmental organizations, and newspapers and is a leading source of research on Brazil.

HISTORY

The São Francisco de Assisi church stands above the historic town of Ouro Preto, or Black Gold. In the 18th century, Ouro Preto was the center of a gold rush. Today the town is known for its baroque art collection and architecture.

2

THE EARLIEST INHABITANTS OF Brazil were the Indians. However, the country's recorded history begins with the arrival of the Portuguese. In 1500, eight years after Christopher Columbus arrived in America, explorer Pedro Álvares Cabral arrived in Brazil.

Cabral had set off from Portugal for India via the coast of Africa. Many previously thought that he found South America by accident, after winds blew him off his path. However, modern historians believe that the Portuguese had already suspected land lay to the west of Africa and sent Cabral to find it.

A picture of native Indian houses in Brazil during the early 18th century.

Historians believe that the first European to discover Brazil, in 1500, was the Portuguese military commander, navigator, and explorer Pedro Álvares Cabral.

An artist's impression of Pedro Álvares Cabral landing at Bay of Porto Seguro in early Brazil.

At that time Spain and Portugal, being Europe's main imperial powers, were sending explorers to the Americas, Africa, and India. On June 7, 1494, Spain and Portugal signed the Treaty of Tordesillas, an agreement that would divide newly discovered lands between them. They drew a line from north to south down the world map and agreed that all lands found to the east of the line would belong to Portugal, whereas all lands found to the west would go to Spain.

When Cabral landed in northeastern Brazil, he stood to the east of the line, giving Portugal a legal claim to part of Spanish America. He sailed to India only two weeks later. Portugal did little to develop its new property, except to send an occasional fleet to collect some *pau brasil* (pow brah-SEEL), a wood from which the Europeans extracted red dye. It was this wood that gave the new colony its name.

EXPANSION IN THE COLONIAL PERIOD

The Portuguese king paid little attention to Brazil until he realized other Europeans would take over the colony if he did not act. He handed out land titles, and in 1534, settlers founded the cities of Olinda and Vitória. The king established a colonial government in the new city of Salvador da Bahia in 1549. In 1567 the Portuguese founded the city of Rio de Janeiro on a site from which they had just expelled a group of French settlers.

According to findings in the state of Piauí, Brazil was inhabited by groups of hunter-gatherers as early as 47,000 years ago. Most experts believe that these hunters made their way from Asia to Brazil via North America. The experts estimate that about 4 million indigenous Indians were living in Brazil when Pedro Álvares Cabral arrived in 1500.

Colonizers from Europe did not bring prosperity and progress to the Indians. Instead the Portuguese unwittingly infected and killed thousands of Indians with new diseases such as measles and smallpox. The Portuguese also tried to force the Indians to work on sugar plantations. Unable to resist the colonizers, many Indians fled to the interior. Those who remained on the coast assimilated into society by marrying Portuguese colonists and African slaves. Today only about 220,000 Indians survive; almost all live in the Amazonian region.

In 1580 politics again boosted Brazil's development. Portugal became part of Spain, making Brazil a target for Spain's enemies Holland and France. The Dutch invaded and conquered parts of the northeastern coast between 1630 and 1654, whereas the French briefly seized what is now the state of Maranhão. The challenge of expelling the invaders brought more people to the colony. In 1625, 70 ships carrying more than 12,000 men sailed from Portugal to help the inhabitants fight the Dutch.

The growing number of settlers spurred the exploration of Brazil's interior. Brazilian colonial scouts known as frontiersmen or *bandeirantes* (bahn-day-RAHN-tehs) took part in exploration expeditions and led marches as far south as Argentina, as far west as Bolivia, and as far north as the Amazon River. The *bandeirantes* established Brazil's claim to lands far west of the Treaty of Tordesillas.

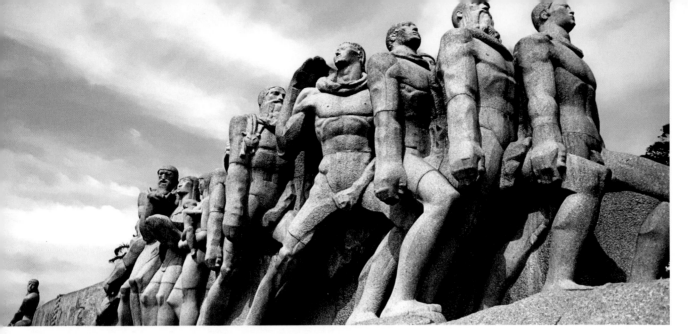

The monument to the *bandeirantes* in São Paulo. The *bandeirantes* were considered all-purpose frontiersmen. They usually had European fathers and Indian mothers. From his Indian heritage, the *bandeirante* had superb scouting and survival skills; from his European side, his desire for wealth and adventure sent him roaming the country.

THE *BANDEIRANTES*

When the *bandeirantes* set off from São Vincente (modern-day São Paulo) at the end of the 16th century, their main purpose was to capture Indians to sell as slaves to plantation owners. The Indians of the northeast fled inland to escape the *bandeirantes*. Ironically, the *bandeirantes* depended on the Indians to guide them on their trips. Some groups of Indians helped the hunters capture rival groups.

Antônio Raposo Tavares (1598—1658) was one of the most notorious *bandeirantes*. In 1628 he set off from São Vincente with 2,000 allied Indians, 900 mestizos (people of European and Indian parentage), and 69 white residents of São Vincente to find precious metals and stones, to capture Indians for slavery, or both. He destroyed several Jesuit missions along the Paraguayan border, resulting in the enslavement of more than 60,000 indigenous people of Spanish Guairá. He then proceeded north along the Paraguay River, until he reached territories that now lie in Bolivia. From there, he followed the Madeira River and then the Amazon, until he reached the Atlantic. In 1651, after traveling more than 3,000 miles (4,828 km), he returned with only 60 men.

After Brazil began transporting African slaves to work on the plantations, the *bandeirantes* began prospecting for gold. They found it in Minas Gerais in 1693, setting off a gold rush that drew thousands of settlers to Brazil's center.

SLAVERY IN BRAZIL

Slaves from Africa played just as big a part in Brazil's development as Portuguese colonists did. Slaves began arriving in the beginning of the colonial times in 1532, and slavery continued up to 1888. At the time of independence in 1822 an estimated 2 million slaves made up more than half of the population. The slaves did not submit willingly to their fate. Many escaped from their masters to the unsettled hills of the interior, where they formed independent colonies called quilombos *(kee-LOHM-boos). The most famous, Quilombo dos Palmares, had a population of 30,000. It survived for 76 years before it was crushed in 1694.*

After Brazil gained independence, a movement to end slavery slowly grew. There were 1,715,000 slaves in 1864. In 1871 while her father was away, the emperor's daughter Princess Isabel convinced the Brazilian congress to grant freedom at birth to the children of slaves. In 1887 there were 723,419 slaves in Brazil. In 1888 the remaining slaves were finally given their freedom. Although there were many free Afro-Brazilian slaves at the time of their liberation, Brazil was the last country in the Western Hemisphere to abolish slavery.

INDEPENDENCE AND EMPIRE

Events in Europe set the stage for Brazil's independence. In 1807 Napoleon's army conquered Portugal. King João VI fled to Rio de Janeiro, making Brazil the only colony ever to become the seat of power for an empire. Before returning to Portugal 14 years later, King João established an effective system of government and left his son, Dom Pedro, to rule Brazil. When King João returned to Portugal, he found a hostile parliament insisting that Brazil be ruled from Lisbon. It also demanded the return of Dom Pedro to Portugal. Judging that the Brazilians would fight for independence rather than return to colonial status, Dom Pedro decided to stay. On September 7, 1822, he proclaimed Brazil's independence. After three months, he was crowned the "constitutional emperor and perpetual defender" of Latin America's only empire.

Emperor Dom Pedro II. This extraordinary but humble man brought much-needed peace to Brazil, giving it the longest period of political stability. He did not adopt the autocratic ways of his father but guided the nation with personal authority. Sadly, Brazil's most popular leader was forced into exile in 1889 when the military overthrew his government.

The perpetual defender lasted only nine years. Brazilians wanted more popular participation in government, but Dom Pedro ruled as an absolute monarch. He fought constantly with the new Brazilian congress and lost popular support when Brazil lost southern territories in a war against Argentina. In 1831 Dom Pedro abdicated and returned to Portugal. He left behind as heir his five-year-old son, Dom Pedro II.

REIGN OF DOM PEDRO II

Following Dom Pedro's departure, rebellion broke out in the northeast and the south, and the country appeared to be on the brink of disintegration. In 1840 the congress turned in desperation to Dom Pedro II, and the 14-year old was crowned emperor of Brazil on July 18, 1841.

Incredibly, Dom Pedro II proved equal to the task. His 48-year rule marked the most stable and progressive stretch in Brazil's history. He granted more power to the congress but used his authority and personal prestige to keep the upper hand in government.

The emperor encouraged agricultural growth and immigration. As a result, by 1888 more than 100,000 Europeans were immigrating annually to southeastern Brazil. Most of them went to work on coffee plantations in São Paulo, since coffee production by that time was responsible for more than half of the country's exports.

Dom Pedro II also promoted education, health, and welfare. His most important achievement was the abolition of slavery in 1888. Dom Pedro II firmly established Brazil's southern borders through battles with neighboring countries. The hardest struggle started in 1865. It took five years for Brazil, allied with Uruguay and Argentina, to defeat Paraguay in this war.

These military campaigns increased the size and stature of the Brazilian army. Military officers became more powerful and began to involve themselves in politics, a development that led to the abolition of the slave trade and eventually to the emperor's downfall. In the 20th century, the military would become Brazil's most powerful political institution.

THE REPUBLIC

The prosperous era of Dom Pedro II ended after a military coup on November 15, 1889. Having lost the support of the landowners through the abolition of slavery, he could not resist a revolt led by the military. He went into exile, and the military proclaimed a new republic of the United States of Brazil. Forty disorderly years followed. The republic had a president and a congress as well as regular elections. Conflicting regional interests made their jobs difficult, however, and the military continued to play an active role in politics. Between 1889 and 1930, 13 presidents held office.

In 1930 a military coup placed Getúlio Vargas, a civilian from the state of Rio Grande do Sul, in the presidency. He represented a new kind of leader: a populist who depended on the support of the urban masses instead of the rich landowners. Vargas legalized labor unions, passed a minimum-wage law, and instituted a social-security system. He also made himself a dictator, first by rewriting the constitution, then by canceling elections. In 1945 the military ousted him and restored democracy. He was reelected president in 1951 and was succeeded in 1954 by Juscelino Kubitschek.

Getúlio Vargas represented a break from Brazil's rural-controlled politics. Instead Brazilian politics began to be dominated by people from the fast-growing urban areas.

Brazilian rancher, lawyer, and dictator-president Getúlio Vargas giving a speech in 1930.

When Brazil declared war on Germany in 1942 it became the first South American country to enter the conflict. The 25,000-strong Brazilian Expeditionary Force (BEF) that went to fight for the Allies in Italy in 1944 was the first South American army to engage in battle overseas. The force served until the end of the war under the command of the U.S. Fifth Army.

Another contribution was the airfield in Natal, in the northeast. Most aircraft at that time could not fly nonstop across the Atlantic. In 1942 U.S. planes stopped at Natal on their way to providing supplies to Allied troops in North Africa, the Middle East, and China.

Brazil entered the war because it felt that with its size and resources, it needed to play a role in world affairs. The country made worthy and immensely vital contributions to the ending of the war.

MILITARY RULE

In the 1950s vast sums of money were spent on building Brasília, hydroelectric plants, highways, and other economic projects. This set the stage for future growth, but it also brought immediate economic problems by plunging the nation into debt. Another coup followed, but this time the military retained power. From 1964 to 1985 Brazil was ruled by a succession of five army generals. In the 1970s Brazil was known for its economic development, when industry grew at a spectacular rate and provided thousands of jobs. Political freedom disappeared, however, and thousands of people were forced into exile or arrested on political grounds.

The economy experienced hyperinflation in the 1980s through to the mid-1990s, and Brazil again was unable to pay back its loans. Frustrated by the debt and by growing public discontent, the military handed power back to a civilian government in 1985. In 1998 Fernando Henrique Cardoso was reelected after his first victory in 1995. The Cardoso government transformed the economy by minimizing the hold of the state on the economy. It redistributed private lands to the poor and privatized many areas of industry previously owned by the state, including telecommunications, oil, mining, and electricity. Cardoso was reelected in 1998 but was confronted with a severe economic crisis, which forced him to appeal to the IMF for aid.

BRAZIL IN THE 21ST CENTURY

In 2003, Luiz da Silva—a member of the opposition Workers' Party—was elected to the presidency. Da Silva's presidency marked a significant point in Brazilian democracy, as it was the first transfer of power between elected presidents since 1961. Da Silva's government was criticized for a series of corruption scandals, but during the presidential elections of 2006, da Silva won by securing 60 percent of the votes, and by 2008 the government successfully reduced Brazil's significant national debt. Da Silva served for eight years and was succeeded by Dilma Rousseff, who was inaugurated as Brazil's first female president in January 2011.

INTERNET LINKS

www.historyworld.net/wrldhis/PlainTextHistories.asp?historyid=aa88

This website provides an in-depth history of Brazil from the 16th to 18th centuries, featuring the Tordesillas Line and revolutionary leader Tiradentes, followed by events of the 19th century including the rule of Pedro I and Pedro II, ending with a focus on 20th-century topics such as Brasília and military rule.

www.countriesquest.com/south_america/brazil/history/independence.htm

Comprehensive coverage of Brazil's journey to independence is presented in this website.

www.geographia.com/brazil/brazihistory.htm

This website provides a short overview of the history of Brazil starting with the Portuguese settlement.

GOVERNMENT

Designed by Oscar Niemeyer, the National Congress of Brazil (Congresso Nacional do Brasil) in Brasília houses Brazil's federal government.

3

B RAZIL IS A FEDERAL REPUBLIC under the leadership of a president whose powers are similar to those of the president of the United States.

THE NEW REPUBLIC

During Brazil's years of military rule from 1964 to 1985, the army had almost complete control of the government, and the congress wielded little power. The military took over the government in 1964 because it believed the president planned to make himself a communist dictator. Since 1985, however, the government of Brazil has been in the hands of civilians; Brazil is said to have entered the era of the "New Republic."

In the New Republic, political power lies in the hands of the president and the congress. The president needs congressional approval for many acts, but like the president of the United States, he or she can veto laws passed by the congress. The president also plays an important role in state politics and has the power to intervene in state affairs, calling in federal troops if necessary. The president is supported by a vice president and a cabinet of state ministers.

As the states cannot levy taxes on their own, they depend on the president to finance their budgets. In 2011, as part of her program of tax reforms, President Dilma Rousseff proposed plans to limit or outlaw states from offering tax exemptions on imports in an effort to stimulate domestic industry. A reduction in payroll taxes for certain industries and a decrease in levies on investments and small companies were also included in the reforms.

Since Brazil gained independence in 1822 its constitution has been rewritten seven times. The constitution of October 1988 contained a

THE BASICS OF GOVERNMENT

Brazil is a federal republic made up of 26 states and the Federal District of Brasília. The government is divided into the executive, legislative, and judicial branches. The president and the cabinet make up the executive branch. The president serves a four-year term with the right to be reelected for an additional four years.

The legislature consists of a congress divided into two bodies: the Senate and the Chamber of Deputies. The Senate has 81 members, three elected from each state and Brasília, whereas the Chamber of Deputies has 513 deputies, with at least three from each state. Senators serve eight-year terms, whereas deputies hold office for four years. Both can run for reelection. Each state has a democratically elected governor and legislature. States are divided into counties called municipios *(moo-nee-SEE-pee-ohs), or municipalities, each of which has an elected mayor and a local council.*

In the judiciary, an 11-member Supreme Federal Tribunal (STF) has the final say in all legal matters. Federal and state courts fall below the STF. Special federal courts handle cases involving labor, military, juvenile, and election issues. Since 2002 all court meetings have been broadcast on television. Brazil's supreme court is one of the busiest in the world; it received more than 100,000 cases in 2010.

The 1988 constitution protects several rights for citizens: freedom of speech, freedom of the press, freedom to assemble peacefully, and freedom for workers to go on strike. It also permits citizens to require the government to release all information it has gathered on them. The latest change in the constitution gave Indians full rights as citizens for the first time and guaranteed Indian groups the rights to all resources falling within their land.

clause requiring a poll to be conducted in 1993 to decide whether to switch from a presidential system of government to a parliamentary system.

In April 1993 a referendum was held to decide the issue. Results showed that almost 70 percent of all votes cast were in favor of retaining the presidential system of government.

ARMY COLONELS

Two types of colonels complicate Brazil's democracy. The first are officers of the military. In the past 100 years, the military has become Brazil's strongest

political institution. All officers are taught that it is their duty to ensure the nation's security; in the past they have intervened in instances they considered a threat to law and order.

Since the 1940s the military has stood watch against any movement connected in the slightest way with communism. After 21 years in power, the military gave up the presidency to a civilian in 1985, publicly guaranteeing that it would not get involved in politics again. However, Brazilians know that the threat of intervention still exists.

HONORARY COLONELS

The second type of colonel has nothing to do with the military. The title of honorary colonel derives from the government's dependence on the National Guard in 1850 to maintain law and order in Brazil's northeast. The wealthy landowners competed for the prestige of being named the colonel in charge.

These colonels became the most important political leaders in their counties. They were the chief law enforcers and supervisors of general elections. They also served as the government's main source of local news as well as its main supporter in the region. They became the intermediaries between the government, which depended on them to deliver election votes, and the voters, who depended on them to get what they needed from the government.

Brazilian president Dilma Rousseff and vice president Michel Temer walk up the main ramp of Palácio do Planalto after their inauguration in Brasília. Lining the entrance are the Army's Presidential Battalion, known as the Dragoons of Independence, wearing a style of ceremonial uniform that dates back to Brazil's independence from Portugal.

As time passed, the National Guard lost its importance, and its colonels disappeared. The wealthiest and most influential men in various counties, however, continue to be called colonels.

These honorary colonels are still the main link between the capital and the countryside. They marshal votes for the governor, who repays their district with special favors. In a land of little education and low pay, citizens often vote for the colonel's candidates because they believe if they help the colonel, he may return the favor.

POLITICAL AWARENESS

The honorary colonels have dominated Brazilian politics for more than 150 years. However, there are signs that their importance is fading.

Most Brazilians now live in cities, so the rural vote has lost some of its importance. The colonels also associated themselves with the military government, and they then lost prestige when the army generals gave up power. Finally, the growth of the media has made it harder for the colonels to manipulate voters.

Before the spread of radio and television, Brazilians living outside the cities knew only the local news. Because the colonels dominated the news, people usually saw fit to vote as the colonels wished. Now they are more aware of national issues and of people who are more powerful.

Previously candidates for election could reach voters only through the colonels. Now they can speak directly to all via radio and television. This has led to the growth of national political parties, the largest being the Brazilian Democratic Movement Party (Partido do Movimento Democrático Brasileiro, or PMDB).

Nearly all literate Brazilians between the ages of 18 and 70 are obliged to vote. Teenagers aged 16 and 17 can vote if they wish. Voting is also voluntary for senior citizens over 70 years old, illiterate people, and prisoners in jail. In Brazil military recruits do not vote. Introduced in 1996, electronic voting, which uses electronic voting booths, set up primarily in banks and bus and train stations, is generally acknowledged to have reduced fraud. By 2000 all precincts were using Brazil's portable electronic voting machines, called *urnas* (a-NARS). Voters punch in digits to select their candidate and confirm their votes by pressing a green button. Brazil has won praise for its affordable and transparent voting-machine system. Although most Brazilians agree that this system is faster and more accessible, others fear that it is open to human and technical failures.

PATRONAGE

In modern Brazil politics still revolves around people, not parties. An example of this took place in the 1989 elections, when the PMDB candidate finished far behind Fernando Afonso Collor de Mello, who overcame the weakness of his party with his charismatic personality and was able to impress voters and form alliances with local leaders.

In the eyes of voters, having friends in the right places is generally more useful than having good ideas. Leaders with good ideas are not good candidates if they cannot get anything done. Moreover, to get things done, they have to know people and be able to make deals.

INTERNET LINKS

www.v-brazil.com/government

This Brazilian website provides information about the judiciary, executive, and legislative branches, including facts about Brazil's political parties and its laws.

www.nationsencyclopedia.com/Americas/Brazil-JUDICIAL-SYSTEM.html

This website provides useful and concise information about Brazil's legal and jury system.

www.countrystudies.us/brazil/82.htm

This website provides in-depth information about the politics and government of Brazil, covering political culture, constitutional framework, government structure, and many other related topics.

Brazilians tell of one town in the state of Pernambuco that has been run by the same family since 1848. At the start of the 1980s, the mayor was the cousin of the district judge, who was the cousin of the civil registrar, who was the cousin of the former public prosecutor, who was the cousin of the district's congressman.

ECONOMY

Logged timber from the Amazon rain forest being loaded onto a ship for export.

4

THE BRAZILIAN ECONOMY BOOMED in the 1970s. The growth rate from 1970 to 1979 reached 8.9 percent. Brazilians believed at that time that their country was destined to be a major world power. The sleeping giant, they said, had finally awoken.

During the years of the "Brazilian miracle," the government spent billions of dollars on large-scale projects such as the Trans-Amazon Highway, subways for Rio de Janeiro and São Paulo, and a nuclear power plant. Most of these were financed by loans from foreign banks. Because of these projects, Brazil experienced spectacular growth.

Brazil is the world's largest soybean producer. Where a rain forest once grew, soybeans are now grown, intended as biofuel or food for humans and livestock.

In the early 1980s to the early 1990s, however, recession hit Brazil, inflation soared, and Brazil's economy ran into trouble. One of the greatest problems facing Brazil at that time was how to pay off its enormous foreign debt. Between 1981 and 1992, the economy of Brazil experienced stagnation. Real gross domestic product (GDP) grew by an average rate of only 1.4 percent, and per capita income decreased by 6 percent. This period is known as the "lost decade." After impressive economic growth in 2007 Brazil experienced a slowdown in the latter half of 2008. This was a result of the global financial crisis decreasing the world's demand for Brazilian exports. Brazil was quick to recover, however, and today Brazil is one of the most successful economies globally, with an impressive average GDP growth rate of 7.5 percent in 2010.

In 2009 the World Economic Forum named Brazil as one of the top countries in terms of economic competitiveness, almost on a par with other major countries such as China and India. A large part of Brazil's success in the past decade can be attributed to private-sector companies being able to develop in a more liberal and open environment. Also aiding Brazil's growth were the effective measures introduced in the 1990s to manage its foreign debt. In 2008 Brazil became a net external creditor for the first time in its history, with total foreign currency assets outnumbering public and private liabilities by $4 billion. In 2010 its public debt figures stood at slightly over 41 percent of its GDP.

INFLATION

Throughout the 1980s, Brazil suffered high inflation rates that almost crippled the economy. In 1990, when annual inflation reached 30,377 percent, the government was forced to rename the currency and reduce its value by a thousand. So 1,000 new cruzados, as the former currency was called, became 1 cruzeiro. Although the government adjusted wages based on inflation, wages and savings still could not keep up. As a result, people looked for ways to avoid losing money. Many converted their cash to U.S. dollars, sometimes at more than twice the official exchange rate. In the past decade, however, inflation in Brazil steadily declined, from 7.6 percent in 2004 to 4.9 percent in 2010.

ECONOMIC PROBLEMS

Brazil's tremendous progress in the past 40 years has improved the lives of many Brazilians. However, there are still millions who live in poverty and do not share in the nation's wealth. Brazilian society is one of the world's most unequal in terms of income distribution. Those in the highest 10 percent of Brazilians receive more than 40 percent of the country's income, whereas the poorest 10 percent receive less than 1 percent. According to the World Bank's 2009 estimates, 21 percent of the population lives below the poverty line.

According to 2007 estimates, in the poorer northeast, people have a life expectancy of 70, whereas for those in the southeast, it is 75. Among children between one and two years old the rate of malnutrition has fallen from 20 percent to 5 percent in Brazil. But northeastern Brazil suffers from a much higher rate of malnutrition. Almost half of all families in the poorer northeastern states live on approximately a dollar a day, and there is widespread hunger.

Every major Brazilian city has its share of slums, called favelas, on the fringes. According to the 2000 census, there were more than 600 favelas in Rio de Janeiro alone. About one-fifth of the residents of Rio de Janeiro live in favelas. By the age of 13, some slum children are on the streets shining shoes, selling gum, begging, or stealing. Children in favelas have little chance of acquiring an education or a well-paid job. Although this pattern is slowly changing, it remains one of the biggest challenges facing Brazil today.

This *garimpeiro* gold mine shows a miners' settlement with the mercury washing pools, deforestation, and pollution.

The Brazilian government successfully reduced the rate of poverty by almost 20 percent between the years 2002 and 2006. This reduction can mainly be attributed to the implementation of major subsidy programs such as Bolsa Família (Family Allowance) and Fome Zero (Zero Hunger), which directly benefited poor families. Bolsa Família provides financial aid to poor families on condition that their children attend school and are vaccinated. Fome Zero guarantees the right of access to basic food for everyone through financial aid, building water cisterns and low-cost restaurants, distributing essential vitamins, and educating people on healthy eating options. Other social programs include Rural Social Security, which provides a financial benefit of one-half of the minimum wage to heads of the family over the age of 65, and Renda Mensal Vitalicia (RMV), which helps those over 70 years old who have no other means of income.

MINERAL WEALTH

Brazil has one of the largest mineral reserves in the world. Brazil ranks second in the world in iron ore reserves, and the recent discovery of platinum in the country could mean it has half of the world's reserves.

Brazil is also a leading producer of bauxite (third in the world), manganese (second in the world), aluminum, cement, ferroalloys (second in the world), tin (seventh in the world), steel (eighth in the world), and gold (13th in the world).

Brazil's most famous gold discovery came in January 1980 at Serra Pelada. Since then, independent miners called *garimpeiros* (gahr-im-PAY-rohs) have been struggling through piles of mud, carrying about 25 tons (25,401 kg) of dirt out of the mine each year.

Gold prospectors have also become rich from the Rondônia and Roraima rivers. Major deposits in the Roraima, along the Venezuelan border, have caused problems, as they are located near the Yanomami Indian reservation. The government has prohibited *garimpeiros* from working there, but so far the lure of gold has outweighed the risk of getting caught.

Besides invading Indian land, the *garimpeiros* cause other problems. They use mercury to separate gold from the soil, thereby polluting the rivers. Working conditions are unhealthy, and the *garimpeiros* suffer from tropical diseases. They also have to look out for tricky businessmen seeking to con them out of their gold.

Still, the mining continues. Brazil produced an estimated 61 tons (62 metric tons) of gold in 2010. In the hills of Pará and along the riverbanks of the Roraima and the Rondônia, hope lives. *Garimpeiros* believe that anyone can become rich with the right combination of hard work and luck.

FARMLAND

One of the world's largest agricultural nations, Brazil produces coffee, soybeans, wheat, rice, corn, sugarcane, cocoa, citrus, and beef.

The country's agricultural sector contributes about 6 percent of total GDP. Raising cattle is a major farming activity in the northeast and the south. Brazil has the largest commercial cattle herd in the world, with export revenues exceeding $1 billion annually.

A pregnant mother with her two daughters in front of their shack in a shantytown. The family lives by collecting, separating, and selling recycled waste.

Since the 1950s, the government has tried to encourage people to move to the country's interior, both to make its borders secure and to reduce overcrowding in settled areas. When the government offered 100 acres (about 0.4 square km) of land to the settlers in Rondônia, it quickly had a waiting list of tens of thousands of families, resulting in the movement of about a million people to Rondônia. Wealthy landowners established huge farms and ranches from this government initiative.

Land ownership is a big issue in Brazil. About 18.8 percent of all Brazilians live in the countryside, but few till their own land. Farm workers are represented by Confederação Nacional dos Trabalhadores na Agricultura (CONTAG), the largest federation of agricultural workers' unions in Brazil. About 1.6 percent of the population owns 46.8 percent of the country's farmland. Workers over 65 years of age in rural areas receive Rural Social Security payments from the government, but rural poverty persists, and more than 12 million landless people are believed to live below the poverty line. The figure used to be higher, but the government has tried to redistribute land wealth by implementing a law that allows it to buy unused private property to give to those who do not own land. However, this law has not been received well on either side of the dispute. Landowners feel the government's payment falls far below the value of their property, whereas peasants feel the government is too slow in enforcing this law. Some peasants have tried occupying unused property illegally, often led by the Landless Workers' Movement, and landowners have responded by hiring gunmen to keep intruders out. The decades-long conflict over land ownership in Brazil has resulted in the loss of thousands of lives.

INDUSTRY

Brazil's industries have grown considerably in the past 35 years. In recent times, many previously state-owned companies in key industries, such as oil, steel, communications, and electricity, have been privatized. In 2009 its automotive industry was the sixth largest in the world. Other sectors that have contributed to employment and industrial development are food and beverages, tobacco, petrochemicals, clothing and footwear manufacturing, cement, and electrical and electronics.

Industrial development has boosted Brazil's exports. While imports amounted to $187.7 billion, exports totaled $199.7 billion in 2010.

INTERNET LINKS

www.cia.gov/library/publications/the-world-factbook/geos/br.html

The CIA World Factbook's economy section provides detailed facts and information about Brazil's current economic situation and an up-to-date overview.

www.reuters.com/article/2010/11/19/us-brazil-summit-economy-idUSTRE6AI3ZZ20101119

The Reuters website provides key facts about the Brazilian economy with information about the country's fiscal policy, major exports, foreign investment, and other economic issues.

www.economywatch.com/world_economy/brazil/

The Economy Watch website provides a brief economic profile with analysis on the country's GDP. It also offers a comprehensive account of Brazil's economic forecast and investment opportunities, as well as statistics on its economic activities.

www.brazil.org.uk/economy/index.html

This official website of the Embassy of Brazil in London provides a useful section on economy and trade, covering foreign trade, capital markets, economic data, and more.

ENVIRONMENT

The Pantanal in Mato Grosso is the world's largest wetlands habitat, hosting almost 1,000 species of land animals and aquatic birds.

5

BRAZIL IS THE FIFTH-LARGEST country in the world. The Amazon River is the second-longest and the Amazon rain forest is the largest in the world. Brazil is one of the most biologically diverse countries in the world and the most diverse in South America, but Brazil is also a land where environmental concerns lead to both peaceful demonstrations and violent battles for control of an area.

NATURE'S RICHES PILED HIGH

Because Brazil is a large and ecologically varied country, it is perhaps not surprising that it ranks as one of the world's most biologically diverse areas in the sheer number of plant and animal species. The country has the largest number of species of primates—the order that includes humans—and ranks first in the number of plant and amphibian species.

Brazil ranks third in the world in the number of bird species and fifth in the number of butterfly and reptilian species. Brazilian flora and fauna live in a variety of environments, including dry forests, rain forests, mountain and lowland forests, marshes, semiarid scrublands, and savannas.

As well as having many ecosystems and a wide variety of plants and animals, Brazil has many species of flora and fauna that are found nowhere else on the planet. The implication of so many unique species

Brazil has signed the following international agreements: Antarctic-Environmental Protocol; Antarctic-Marine Living Resources; Antarctic Seals; Antarctic Treaty; Biodiversity; Climate Change; Climate Change-Kyoto Protocol; Desertification; Endangered Species; Environmental Modification; Hazardous Wastes; Law of the Sea; Marine Dumping; Ozone Layer Protection; Ship Pollution; Tropical Timber 83; Tropical Timber 94; Wetlands; and Whaling.

Located in southwestern Paraná, Iguaçú covers 420,291 acres (170,086 ha) of protected area. A total of 90 percent of the park is subtropical rain forest, where plants such as tree ferns, liana vines, and epiphytes flourish. Epiphytes are plants that can grow without roots. The seeds attach themselves to the branches of trees, and the growing plants absorb moisture and nutrients directly from the air, without harming the host tree. Animals in Iguaçú include the ocelot, the jaguar, the puma, the giant otter, the American tapir, the bush dog, the giant anteater, the broad-nosed caiman, and a variety of birds, such as the harpy eagle. Both the glaucous macaw and the black-fronted piping-guan are local birds on the endangered list.

The Iguaçú National Park was named a World Heritage Site in 1986, partly because it contains the Brazilian share of the Iguaçú Falls (below). This fantastic waterfall is one of the world's largest and extends over a 2-mile (3-km) area. The water drops 269 feet (82 m) down a giant stairway, and the mist created keeps the surrounding land and the islands in the river covered in lush vegetation. Although the park is a protected site,

it is threatened by poachers and people who raid the forests looking for palm trees that produce palm hearts used in salads. Between 1999 and 2001 the park was listed as endangered by the World Heritage Site.

The Iguaçú Falls were featured in the 1986 movie The Mission, about the Jesuits who tried to protect Guaraní Indians from Brazilian slave raiders in the 1700s.

is that environmental protection here is far more important than in countries that host more common plants and animals.

Brazil hosted the United Nations Conference on the Environment and Development—more commonly known as the Earth Day Summit—in Rio de Janeiro in 1992 and negotiated agreements on sustainable development. It will host the Rio Plus 20 global environmental summit in 2012. However, there have been laws protecting wildlife, forests, and waterways in the country since the 1930s, long before the summit put Brazil on the environmental map.

The constitution provides for environmental protection measures that are advanced in comparison with those of many other countries. There are several government bodies looking out for the environment, such as the Ministry of Environment and the Institute for the Environment and Renewable Natural Resources.

In addition to these government bodies, there are a number of nongovernmental organizations working to protect the environment, including the SOS Atlantic Rain Forest Foundation, dedicated to preserving the Atlantic rain forest ecosystem, and the Amazon Working Group, dedicated to the Amazon River Basin and forest. Aliança da Terra, established by an American-born cattle rancher in 2004, works with farmers to promote sustainable ways of managing the rain forest, thereby delaying the pace of deforestation. Other nongovernmental organizations include the Projeto TAMAR, a nonprofit organization whose main objective is to protect sea turtles along the Brazilian coastline from extinction.

Brazilians are aware of the natural treasures within their national borders. There are laws protecting forests and wildlife, and there are people dedicated to putting these laws to use.

CHALLENGES

Brazil faces many serious environmental threats. The best known of these is the destruction of the Amazon rain forest, the earth's lungs. Between 1990 and 1999 approximately 63,000 square miles (163,169 square km) of forest were destroyed. A single burning season in 1995 resulted in the deforestation of 11,197 square miles (29,000 square km) of the Amazon forest—almost the size of Maryland.

Contrary to popular belief, most of the deforestation then was done by large commercial interests rather than by impoverished peasants. The government at the time encouraged economic growth through expansion of land under agricultural production, and that meant large swaths of

The SOS Atlantic Rain Forest Foundation is a nonprofit organization established in 1986 with the goal of protecting what is left of Brazil's Atlantic rain forest and the Indian groups who live in the area.

SAVING THE RAIN FOREST: WHAT'S ALL THE FUSS ABOUT?

Many people are aware of the urgent need to protect the world's forests, especially the Amazon. However, few understand exactly why these forests are so important, except that they are home to beautiful animals and plants. There are many reasons to protect the forests, but perhaps one of the most important is that they are the lungs of the planet.

As the sun warms the earth, the earth radiates some of the sun's heat back into space. Greenhouse gases, such as carbon dioxide, methane, nitrous oxide, and ozone, retain heat in the earth's atmosphere. (Nitrogen and oxygen, which make up most of our air, do not retain heat.) The planet needs small amounts of these greenhouse gases to provide a hospitable environment for life.

Before people began using fossil fuels and burning up forests, the forests were a key part of the equation in maintaining a balance between heat-retaining and other gases. Volcanic activity produced most of the carbon dioxide, which forests absorbed and converted into oxygen and cellulose.

Today the rain forests remain important, but we face two related problems: About half of the forests are gone, and industrial activity has released billions of tons of additional carbon dioxide into the atmosphere. This means more heat is retained in the atmosphere, leading to global warming. Scientists predict that there will be a 6.3ºF (11.3ºC) overall warming of the atmosphere by the end of the 21st century, with 2005 having been the hottest year in the history of the planet so far. This warming trend could have disastrous results, including the melting of polar ice caps and the flooding of coastlines (where about 50 percent of all people live). Drastic changes in weather patterns will alter environments, leading to widespread extinction of plants and animals.

The two major sources of carbon dioxide are the burning of forests and the use of fossil fuels, which produce nearly 23 and 77 percent, respectively, of all carbon dioxide emissions. Brazil is the biggest culprit for forest burning, but the United States is the world's largest contributor of greenhouse gases, producing 22 percent of all greenhouse-gas emissions. To help the planet "breathe" and keep our environment healthy for life, the Amazon has to be preserved and greenhouse-gas emissions reduced.

forest were made available to those who were willing to burn it down and make pasture for cattle. Deforestation continued even in later years, when economic crises and slowdowns reduced the rate of forest clearing and public

The Belo Monte Dam is a proposed hydroelectric dam complex on the Xingu River in the Brazilian state of Pará. The proposed size of its reservoir is approximately 258 square miles (668 square km), which will make it the third largest in the world.

The plans, in existence since 1975, have been supported by the government but open to much public controversy in spite of the launch of a new design in the 2000s. In 2011 an installation license was granted, but it was quickly revoked by a federal judge before construction could begin. This was later overturned to allow work to progress on the dam.

Those who oppose the construction of the dam have a wide-ranging list of environmental and social concerns, including the destruction of the Amazon's biodiversity and natural landscape, permanent flooding, damage to the water supply, threat to the survival of the indigenous people, displacement of 20,000 people, and pressure to provide employment and other services to meet the needs of an increased population in the area.

opinion against this strategy began to grow. Between 2000 and 2010 the situation had worsened, and approximately 71,000 square miles (183,889 square km) of forest were lost. The deforestation rate for Brazil's Amazon is between 6,564 square miles (17,000 square km) and 30,888 square miles (80,000 square km) per year.

Other areas in Brazil, such as the dry northeast, are also under threat from human activities. Clearing land in the northeast for cattle has resulted in soil erosion and desertification. The Atlantic forests are nearly gone, and several plants and animals that are unique to this ecosystem now face extinction. Mining activities all over the country result in land degradation and water pollution. Gold mining in particular relies on the use of poisonous substances

LAND USE: AN ENVIRONMENTALLY SOUND ANSWER?

Brazil is a country with vast resources, both natural and human. Land is used for cattle-rearing as well as agriculture, including the growing of crops such as coffee, corn, rice, and wheat.

Unfortunately its history has created a situation in which only a few people own most of the farmland even though they are often not the people cultivating it. In the meantime, the government has tried to resettle millions of landless rural workers onto newly cleared plots in the rain forest. This means that more forested land is being lost. Furthermore, since tropical soils are poor for agriculture, most small farmers end up abandoning their plots of land after a few years of trying to cultivate them.

The Landless Workers' Movement has organized thousands of rural families to occupy unused farmland, make it productive, and then claim legal ownership of the land in the courts. Since 1985, when the Catholic Church began to help organize poor rural people, the Landless Workers' Movement helped more than 250,000 families occupy and gain title to more than 15 million acres (60,703 square km) of farmland. In 2005 a grueling 79-mile (127-km) march organized by the members of the movement put pressure on then-President Lula to promise the resettlement of 430,000 landless families.

The movement has won international awards for its environmentally sound projects and educational efforts. Once families form a new community on occupied land, they start a school, and the movement helps them find teachers for the children and tutors for the illiterate adults. The movement claims that between 2002 and 2005, more than 50,000 landless workers have been taught reading and writing.

Landowners who are unhappy with the movement have hired mercenaries to kill potential settlers, and more than 1,000 people have lost their lives. Most Brazilians, however, support the movement, although some, including the government, have their reservations about its methods.

such as mercury and cyanide to separate the gold from silt. Damaging the environment is not restricted to rural areas. Due to overcrowding and inadequate facilities, cities generate huge amounts of air and water pollution.

In recent years, Brazil has suffered severe droughts. The drought in 2005 was so extreme that scientists called it a "once in a century" event. In 2010 Brazil suffered yet another harsh drought, which killed millions of trees. The destruction of trees is worrying, as it reduces the ability of the Amazon rain forest to absorb carbon dioxide emissions. Scientists are concerned that Brazil will continue to experience extreme droughts in the future.

SOLUTIONS

There are Brazilian organizations that are working to find a way to save the Amazon from human rampage. However, they will be more likely to succeed if wealthy countries help Brazil to find more environmentally sound methods of creating energy and maintaining jobs and lifestyles.

> The Amazon rain forest accounts for more than 95 percent of Brazil's remaining forests, and 10 percent of the Amazon has already been cleared for cattle ranching, mining, and hydroelectricity projects.

INTERNET LINKS

www.mma.gov.br/sitio/en

The official website of Brazil's Ministry of Environment provides information on ways in which Brazil is promoting principles and strategies to protect the country's environment.

www.greenpeace.org/international/en/campaigns/forests/amazon/amazon-flora-and-fauna/

This official website of Greenpeace International provides information about the abundant and diverse flora and fauna found in Brazil and a general overview of life in the Amazon.

www.worldheritagesite.org/sites/iguacunationalpark.html

This World Heritage website provides comprehensive information on Brazil's stunning Iguaçú National Park with reviews from visitors.

BRAZILIANS

A Brazilian boy in Pelourinho, or the old town, in Salvador.

APART FROM ISOLATED GROUPS OF indigenous Indians in the Amazon and recent immigrants from Europe and Asia, most Brazilians are either Caucasian or of mixed ethnicity.

Children of African and European parents are called *morenos* (mo-RAY-nohs) or mulattos—people from mixed black and white ancestry. *Caboclo* (kah-BOH-cloh) children have European and Indian blood, and children of African and Indian parents are called *cafusos* (kah-FOO-sohs). According to 2008 estimates, 48.43 percent of Brazilians are Caucasian, 43.80 percent are multiracial, 6.84 percent are black, 0.58 percent are Asian, 0.28 percent are Amerindian, and 0.07 percent are unspecified.

Despite being an ethnic melting pot, Brazil is still marked by strong regional differences. In general, the European influence is stronger in the south and the southeast, whereas African culture dominates the states of Bahia and Rio de Janeiro as well as much of the northeast. Indian traditions have left their mark in the *sertão* in the northeast and in the northern and central-western regions.

More and more Brazilians are leaving the countryside to live in the crowded cities, especially São Paulo. As a result, favelas, or slums, sheltering thousands of poor immigrants in unhygienic conditions have grown in almost every large city. About 20 percent of Rio de Janeiro's residents— more than 1 million people—live in favelas.

POPULATION DISTRIBUTION

Brazil's growth rate has slowed in the past decade. From 2008 to 2010, the growth rate decreased from 1.23 percent to 1.17 percent. In 2011, the growth rate was 1.13 percent. Nevertheless, its population

Baiana **women dressed in their traditional costumes in Salvador da Bahia.**

is young, and about 26 percent of Brazilians are below 14 years of age. Brazil has space for a large population if it is spread out, but most people choose or are forced to live in the cities, due to the lack of available land and jobs in the countryside. Some 87 percent of Brazilians live in urban rather than rural areas, and about 20 percent live in one of three cities: São Paulo, Rio de Janeiro, and Belo Horizonte. This creates pressure on cities to find space and provide services for the mushrooming populations.

DISCRIMINATION

Brazil's constitution prohibits racial discrimination, and Brazilians are glad to not have to suffer racial strife in their country. Nonetheless, inequality among ethnic groups is a daily reality.

For example, dark-skinned men or women are rarely found in the congress or among army generals, corporate presidents, or diplomats. The average income and education level of Afro-Brazilians fall far below those of lighter-skinned Brazilians. In 2008, Afro-Brazilians had completed on average 6.5 years of years of schooling, whereas their Caucasian counterparts had received 8.3 years. And of the 10.2 million families enrolled in the Bolsa Família initiative, 66.4 percent were Afro-Brazilians, whereas only 26.8 percent were Caucasian. Nationally almost 25 percent of Afro-Brazilian families received aid from Bolsa Família.

Other evidence to show the gap in the standard of living can be seen in the 6.6-year difference in life expectancy that Brazilians of Caucasian descent enjoy over those of Afro-Brazilian descent. Infant mortality rates are also lower in Caucasian families than in Afro-Brazilian families.

Many argue that this is not the product of racial discrimination. They argue instead that it is a reflection of the lack of opportunities for Afro-Brazilians, most of whom come from the poorer northeast. Whether it is racism or not, most Brazilians associate dark skin with the lower classes. To redress the discrimination, selected universities have adopted affirmative-action admission policies to help Afro-Brazilians access and benefit from higher education.

Nevertheless, Brazilians frequently intermarry, and the number of intermarriages is on the rise. It is believed that during the past 50 years, the number of mulattos or *morenos* has greatly increased, whereas the percentage of whites and blacks in the population has dropped.

More recently, however, there have been changes in the way Afro-Brazilians define or identify themselves in terms of their ethnicity. Only a minority declare themselves to be "black," whereas the majority choose to be "brown."

THE INDIANS

Almost all of Brazil's remaining 200,000 Indians live in the Amazon. The jungle still largely isolates them from the modern world, so that Brazilians face the challenge of integrating Indians into modern society without destroying Indian culture.

In 1961 the government's National Foundation for Assistance to Indians created the Xingu National Park in part to protect the local Indians and introduce modern tools and ideas to them. Some Indians have made the leap to modern society. In 1982 a leader of the Xingu group was elected to the national congress.

Open land and the promise of gold in Indian territories have attracted new settlers, who like the early European colonists bring diseases and unfamiliar ideas with them. Some Indians are fighting to preserve their land and tradition. In 1992, backed by huge international support, the Yanomami won their claim for a reserve three times the size of Belgium. In 1993, 16 Yanomami people were killed in an armed conflict, known as the Haximu Massacre, with a band of gold diggers who were mining the land illegally.

Parrots are favored pets among Xingu Indians in the Amazon. Many younger, educated Indians hope to raise the consciousness of the nation to the plight of some of their people.

Many other Indian groups still face the challenge of preserving their heritage while integrating into mainstream society.

SÃO PAULO: COSMOPOLITAN CENTER

More than any other Brazilian city, São Paulo is a city of immigrants. For the past century, it has attracted the bulk of the country's European and Asian immigrants. From 1960 to 2000, São Paulo's population grew from 3.8 million to 17.7 million. According to the 2010 census, the metropolitan population grew even more, to more than 41 million.

Thousands of migrants, mostly from the northeast, live in the Bras neighborhood. Walking through Bras, you can hear the music of *violeiros* (vee-oh-LAY-roos)—fiddlers who compose songs in response to challenges from their audience—and see street vendors peddling alligator skins and Amazonian herbs.

In the Bom Retiro neighborhood, Muslims, Jews, and Christians—descendants of immigrants from Lebanon, Syria, and Turkey—live peacefully in the thriving Middle Eastern shopping district.

A large proportion of São Paulo's 6 million residents of Italian descent live in the Bela Vista neighborhood, a Little Italy with European-style cantinas.

A unique group of immigrants founded the city of Americana, about an hour's drive from São Paulo. The city's seal tells its history: It features the stars-and-bars insignia of the Confederate States of America, flanked by two soldiers wearing the Confederate Army uniform.

After the end of the American Civil War in 1865, about 3 million Southerners from the defeated Confederate states left America. A handful ended up in Brazil, where they started several settlements. Americana is the most prominent of the surviving settlements.

While most of its current 199,000 residents are descendants of later European immigrants, Americana's Confederate heritage is evident. Walking down the streets, you can very occasionally hear English spoken with a Southern accent. A monument in the downtown area honors Confederate soldiers who died in the Civil War. Nearby stands a cemetery with the graves of Confederate immigrants.

Every August, during a festival held in memory of the homeland, the residents consume 1,300 gallons (5,909 l) of wine, 3 tons (3,048 kg) of spaghetti, and 40,000 pizzas.

Liberdade is home to most of São Paulo's 665,000 residents of Japanese descent. Street signs in this neighborhood advertise in Japanese, and residents and visitors can read three local Japanese newspapers, sign up for judo classes, and dine at Asian restaurants.

FAMOUS BRAZILIANS

EDSON ARANTES DO NASCIMENTO Otherwise known all over the world as Pelé, the legendary Brazilian soccer player and international sporting hero. Born into a poor family, he developed his world-class skills playing soccer with his father, who was also an excellent player.

His talent was discovered at the age of 11 by another of Brazil's famous soccer players, Waldemar de Brito, who confidently declared that Pelé would be "the greatest soccer player in the world." Pelé was greatly admired for his speed, balance, control, and heading ability.

Perhaps the most powerful symbol of Brazil's African heritage, baianos (bah-YAH-nohs) are residents of Bahia, the state with the largest population descended from slaves. In popular usage, baianas (bah-YAH-nahs) refers specifically to Afro-Brazilian women seen selling food on the city streets, wearing the traditional white clothing of their ancestors. They participate in special occasions such as Salvador's Festival of Our Lord of Bonfim and Rio de Janeiro's Carnival.

At only 17 years of age, Pelé played in the 1958 World Cup, where he scored an amazing six goals that led to Brazil's victory. He went on to play in four more World Cups with Brazil's national team.

Throughout his amazing career, Pelé scored 1,280 goals in 1,360 games and holds the world record for hat tricks (92) and the number of goals scored on the international level (97).

He received many accolades after his retirement from "the beautiful game" in 1977. In 1978 he received the International Peace Award, in 1980 he was named athlete of the century, in 1993 he was inducted into the National Soccer Hall of Fame, and in 2000 he came in second for the FIFA Sportsman of the Century award. Apart from his sporting achievements, Pelé has also offered his support to many children's charities.

AYRTON SENNA DA SILVA Ayrton Senna da Silva was a legendary Brazilian motor-racing driver. He is considered to be one of the greatest drivers in the history of Formula One. He became famous for winning the Formula One World Championships three times, in 1988, 1990, and 1991. Sadly, he is also known as the last Grand Prix driver to lose his life at the wheel of a Formula One car, having sustained fatal injuries after a horrific crash at the 1994 San Marino Grand Prix.

Born in 1960 in São Paulo, da Silva fell in love with racing when he was just four years of age. He embarked on his motorsport career in karting. He launched his Formula One career in 1984, and by 1988 he had claimed his first World Championship. In racing circles, da Silva is most admired for his qualifying speed over one lap. Moreover, between 1989 and 2006 he held the record for most pole positions. In addition, his impressive six-time victory at the celebrated Monaco Grand Prix is a world record.

Da Silva's status as a national hero was affirmed when Brazil declared three days of national mourning and a state funeral to mark his untimely death. His funeral, the largest in Brazilian history, was attended by approximately 1 million people.

In addition to his sporting successes, da Silva is remembered for his charitable legacy. He had donated millions of dollars of his personal fortune (estimated at $400 million at the time of his death) to children's charities. Through his foundation, the Instituto Ayrton Senna, almost $80 million has been invested during the past 12 years in social programs aimed at giving young people from poor backgrounds the skills and opportunities they need to develop to their full potential.

Ayrton Senna is widely regarded as one of the greatest Formula One drivers of all time.

INTERNET LINKS

www.indexmundi.com/brazil/

This website provides updated and in-depth facts and statistics about the population of Brazil, showing growth rates from different years.

www.kwintessential.co.uk/articles/article/Brazil/Population-and-People-of-Brazil/74

This website provides useful information about the ethnic groups in Brazil, including Caucasians, mulattos, and Afro-Brazilians.

www.wordiq.com/definition/Indigenous_people_of_Brazil

This website provides detailed information about the indigenous peoples of Brazil, such as the Yanomani, the Ticuna, the Awá, and the Guarani.

LIFESTYLE

Multiethnic Brazilians come together each weekend to shop for goods in São Paulo.

I N BRAZIL, THERE EXISTS A WIDE GAP between the rich and the poor, and this affects lifestyle choices. The affluent in Brazil, like elsewhere in the world, enjoy a high standard of luxury, living in lavish homes, while those in extreme poverty struggle to find work and often live in basic accommodation in favelas, or slums.

However, it would seem that even under the harshest of conditions, many of the poor still have a remarkable ability to enjoy life and be optimistic. Generally, the lifestyle in Brazil tends to be pleasant, free of trouble, and relaxed. An example of this is the way many Brazilians have a flexible approach to timekeeping. When making an appointment

Favelos of Rio de Janeiro as seen from Santa Teresa Hill.

Brazilians are known for their love of life. In general, Brazilians are warm people who enjoy family, friends, food, music, and dancing.

to meet friends for an evening out, it is not uncommon for someone to arrive an hour or more later than the agreed time!

Brazilians' love of life is encapsulated in the passionate way its people celebrate national events, such as soccer matches and the famous annual Carnival. The energetic lifestyle can also be experienced through the lively beats and rhythms of Brazilian dance and music.

"WE'LL FIND A WAY"

In a society where rules are generally quite flexible, getting things done is a tricky, inexact science. *Jeito* (JAY-toh), meaning "way around" or "quick fix," is the word used to describe this science. To Brazilians, the word evokes much. A person called a *jeitoso* (jay-TOH-zoo) is a master at squirming out of difficult situations and solving complicated problems. When most people say some goal is impossible, a *jeitoso* promises to *dar um jeito* (DAH oom JAY-toh), or find a way. The key to *jeito* is knowing when and how to bend the rules. Sometimes the authority behind the rules is strong enough to force compliance. Other times, rules are just pointless obstacles that can, and should, be avoided.

Traffic laws offer a good example of Brazilians' flexible attitude. For Brazilian drivers in cities like Rio de Janeiro, a red traffic light does not always mean "stop." For some, it means "stop" only if there is likely to be traffic. Late at night, when the streets are deserted, some drivers see no reason to stop and rarely do.

In the larger cities, some motorists pull right onto the sidewalk to park. The law prohibits this, of course, and periodically the government embarks on campaigns to keep the sidewalks for pedestrians.

INTERMEDIARIES

Compromise is what keeps life going in Brazil; negotiation is the name of the game. Merchants and customers bargain over prices; taxi drivers and riders haggle over fares. While Brazilians take pride in their skills of negotiation, situations do occasionally arise that require outside help involving mediators.

Brazilian Catholics pray to patron saints, invoking them as allies. When they encounter a problem, they count on a saint to intercede with God on their behalf. The political equivalent to the saint is the colonel. Although declining in influence as Brazil becomes more and more urbanized, the colonel is still the most influential citizen in certain rural communities, and people support the candidate the colonel supports during elections because they know the colonel can get help from the elected person on their behalf.

Businessmen may hire a "fixer," called a *despachante* (dehs-pah-SHAHN-cheh), to deal with routine tasks by navigating the bureaucracy on their behalf. The *despachante* might ask a relative who works for the trade ministry to speed up his employer's application for a license or an influential friend to make phone calls on behalf of his client. Brazilians dislike corruption, but it is a way of getting many things done. It is increasingly fought by organizations such as Transparência Brasil (TrBrasil) and through congressional investigations.

A happy family unit in Brazil.

FAMILY TIES

Bonds with friends and family are very tight in Brazil. Children usually live with their parents at least until they marry. If they do not earn enough to start out on their own, married children continue to live with their parents. Those who move out usually remain close to home and will visit their parents very frequently.

Brazilians also stay in touch with relatives beyond their immediate family. While many young people in the United States have never met their second cousins, in Brazil distant cousins often meet at family gatherings and on other occasions.

Brazil has a social-security system. The elderly receive social security, but some still depend on their children to support them. Although in the past many people believed that having a large number of children was the best guarantee against hardship in old age, some poor parents are unable to support all their children and have no choice but to send them into the streets to find work. At the same time, an improvement in health conditions and changes in attitudes in recent years has led to a decline in Brazilian fertility rates. It was estimated that Brazil had a fertility rate of 2.18 children per woman in 2011.

Godparents are very important in Brazil. A man who agrees to sponsor a child at baptism becomes a *padrinho* (pah-DRIN-hoo) to the child and a *compadre* (kom-PAH-dray) to the child's parents. The first word translates as "little father," and the second can be interpreted as "joint father." A godparent and his family become accepted members of the family of the baptized child, just as if they had married into the family.

FRIENDSHIP

Brazilians have two kinds of friends. Social friends are people you get together with to eat with, dance with, or discuss local news but not to share intimate subjects such as family problems or personal ambitions. Nor do social friends meet in one another's homes. The home is a private place reserved for family members and close friends. Only after many years of friendship can two Brazilians become close friends. The understanding and loyalty involved in this kind of friendship takes a long time to evolve. Most Brazilians have only a handful of close friends, whom they accept as family and whom they know they can count on in any crisis.

Duty demands that relatives and friends help one another in times of need, even if it causes a lot of inconvenience. A city dweller is bound to provide lodging for a visiting distant cousin, regardless of how long he or she stays. A host who suggests that the relative leave or pay rent would be considered rude and ungrateful. A good family member refuses to accept contributions from a visiting relative. To do so would be to reveal that he cannot fulfill his duty. Modern economics and values, however, are gradually changing this.

THE GATHERING OF FRIENDS

Brazilians love to be around other people. They enjoy chatting over drinks and dancing late into the night with friends. They love to have relatives and close friends stop by their homes.

A lot of drinking and conversation usually precedes the main meal whenever Brazilians hold dinner parties. Often the host does not seat the guests until 11 P.M. At no time does the host leave the guests to attend to the preparation of the meal. To do so suggests a lack of respect or inadequate preparation for the guests' arrival. Where possible, servants are employed to prepare the meal; otherwise, the host should prepare everything in advance. Guests may bring a gift of flowers but never food, as the latter suggests that the host needs help entertaining friends.

Brazilian families enjoying a meal together at a country inn near São Paulo.

To maintain the privacy of the home, most Brazilians hold large parties in clubs or community halls. Even parties for teenagers start late, often after 10 P.M., and continue into the early morning hours.

Food, music, and dancing are standard ingredients of festivities. Guests may not necessarily have been invited. Brazilians think nothing of bringing friends or visiting relatives with them to parties. However, strangers should not expect to be introduced to anyone at the party. Formal introductions are considered too stiff for the festive atmosphere. You do not need to know someone's name in order to have a good conversation and a good time.

Brazilians place little emphasis on punctuality. They habitually show up late for both business and social functions. In fact, anyone arriving at a party earlier than a half-hour after the time stated on the invitation is most likely to find an empty room. The early bird may possibly even have arrived before the host. In the rare event that guests are expected to turn up on time, invitations specify the starting time as Swiss Time, British Time, or American Time.

Family members of all ages come together to celebrate the 102nd birthday of this grandmother in Santo Amaro da Purificação.

BIRTHDAYS

In Brazil, birthday parties are mainly a family affair, so children of all ages and adults are invited.

Children's birthday celebrations in Brazil are similar to those in the United States. In larger cities, such as Rio and São Paulo, families may celebrate children's birthdays at *casas de festa*, or party houses. Adults often have small family gatherings, followed by larger parties, to celebrate. Even casual friends make every effort to attend. To miss such an event is to fail in one's duty as a friend.

Upper-class families mark the 15th birthday of a daughter with a big debutante ball. The birthday girl and her closest friends dress in white gowns, and their escorts wear suits or tuxedos. The evening often begins with a Mass, and then guests attend a reception, where a lavish buffet and a live band await. At midnight the guest of honor formally enters society by having one dance with her father, followed by a second with her escort.

WEDDINGS

Before the wedding, the groom and his friends celebrate with a bachelor party at a club. The bridesmaids throw the bride a shower in the kitchen of the bride's best friend's home.

The immediate family attends a small ceremony where civil documents are signed. The main event, the church wedding, then follows. All relatives and family friends attend the Mass and then a large reception. After cutting the wedding cake and bidding farewell to the guests, the newlyweds leave on their honeymoon. An interesting wedding custom, followed only in certain parts of the country, requires the groom to tame an unbridled donkey to prove that he is a worthy husband. If successful, he is deemed suitable to marry the daughter of the donkey's owner.

Owing to the strong opposition of the Catholic Church, divorce was made legal in Brazil only in 1977.

FUNERALS

Families usually bury their dead within 24 hours. News of the funeral travels by word of mouth, and those notified are expected to attend.

Mourners stay up through the night, drinking and trading stories about the deceased.

At a designated time, a hearse carrying the coffin leads a procession to a church, where a requiem is offered. In smaller towns, the body will be buried in the church's private cemetery; in large cities, the procession moves to a larger public cemetery. A Mass is held in memory of the deceased after seven days, 30 days, and a year.

MACHO MEN

Despite changing social trends, Brazil remains a man's country. The husband traditionally earns and manages his family's income, although 60 percent of women were in the labor force in 2008. Women do most of the daily household chores and raise the children in addition to protecting family traditions and social customs.

As do most other South American men, Brazilian men take the lead in courting the women. A man is expected to aggressively pursue the woman he has his eyes on, but a woman who displays too much initiative in approaching men quickly gains a bad reputation.

A strict code of chivalry moderates the pursuit of love. Men are expected to give up their seats on buses and to open doors for women. In a restaurant, some men will seat their date, order for her, and pay the bill. The main feature of machismo is a desire to play a leading role and uphold one's honor. At the same time, Brazilian men do not feel compelled to hide their emotions. They do not hesitate to show affection to women, to hug close friends, or to cry over dying relatives.

The proud and conservative gauchos epitomize Brazilian machismo.

THE GIRLS FROM IPANEMA

Brazilian women are famous around the world for their beauty and charm. "The Girl from Ipanema," a popular song of the 1960s, has become a symbol

of Latin beauty. Enchanted by a typical Brazilian beauty who frequented the famous Ipanema beach in Rio de Janeiro, songwriters Antonio Jobim and Vinicius de Moraes put their feelings to music and came up with a song that became a standard.

Looking good is important to Brazilian women, who seek to be stylish and charming in everything they do. Girls learn to wear jewelry and apply makeup from a young age. On the beach, they wear bathing suits that not only help them get a tan but also encourage them to keep trim.

While the machismo concept makes a man play a dominating role, the Brazilian traditional idea of femininity can promote dependency on others. In the countryside, marriage is still believed to be so essential for feminine self-fulfillment that single women in their 30s are pitied.

A typical Brazilian beauty on Ipanema beach in Rio de Janeiro.

WOMEN'S PLACE IN SOCIETY

The inauguration of Brazil's first female president, Dilma Rousseff, in January 2011 raised the profile of women in Brazil. During the World Economic Forum in 2010 it was announced that gender equality in Brazil had been achieved in the areas of education and health, but women still earned 30 percent less than men. Moreover, in spite of Rousseff's historic presidency, women continue to be underrepresented in the political arena.

Although illegal, domestic violence is rife in Brazil, where many in society, including women, quietly tolerate the violent behavior of men toward their wives and partners. It is believed that in Brazil a woman is beaten by her husband every 15 seconds.

Each year hundreds of wives are beaten, and even killed, because of their husband's jealousy and suspicions. Women rarely report these actions, since the law rarely punishes men for "crimes of passion." A well-known "crime of passion" is the case of Maria da Penha, who became a paraplegic after her husband beat her in 1983. Since then she has become a symbol for Brazilian women who campaign to reduce such violence toward women by their husbands.

Fortunately, things are changing, albeit slowly. Stricter laws have been passed for crimes committed against wives. In 2006 the Maria da Penha Law was sanctioned to ensure such crimes receive the appropriate punishment, which can include imprisonment.

A growing number of women are pursuing careers and participating in activities previously regarded as unfeminine, such as team sports and politics. In 1997 Brazil began a system reserving 30 percent of the membership of each political party for women. Yet there remains a long way to go in achieving gender equality in Brazilian politics. Although women made up 51.5 percent of the electorate in 2006, they accounted for only 8.8 percent of those elected to top positions such as federal deputies.

Women helping their children with their homework in the city of Itaparica.

BRINGING UP CHILDREN

Having a large family and being frequently visited by relatives, Brazilian children are constantly surrounded by loved ones and never left alone. Many families hire nurses to look after the children, and those who cannot afford nurses can always count on help from their relatives.

Babies in particular receive constant attention. They rarely escape the hands of the caregiver, and when they cry they become the center of attention. Sometimes even strangers on the street will stop to offer suggestions to a mother with a crying baby.

Many Brazilian parents pamper their children. Few believe in strict discipline. They may simply send a child out of the room for bad behavior when there are guests, but they usually ignore a child who acts up in church or in a store. They believe it is inevitable that children will get bored or unhappy in a place where there is nothing to entertain them.

Uniformed children in their classroom.

Until they reach the teenage years, children rarely do work around the house. Moreover, upper-class Brazilians do not allow their children to work part-time while they are in school, as they feel that such work suggests to outsiders that the family is in financial trouble. In any case, Brazilian law does not allow children to work until they reach 16 years of age.

In this male-oriented society, boys are treated more leniently than girls. Girls usually cannot stay out late, and their parents do not like them going out without a chaperone. Teenagers usually start dating at around age 17. First dates are not seen as anything serious, since newly dating couples often go out in groups.

EDUCATION

Students in Brazil attend nine years of elementary school between the ages of 6 and 14, followed by three years of high school. According to data collated for the period 2005—09, although student enrollment has risen sharply during the past two decades, only 76 percent of students stay in school through grade 5, the last grade of primary school. Because many poor teenagers have part-time jobs and because of a shortage of classroom space, many high schools hold classes in shifts. Progress is measured in "cycles" or classroom hours rather than school years, so that working students can learn at their own pace. A "cycle" usually represents two years at school.

In Brazil public higher education is provided free, and many of the best universities are public. In 2009 it was estimated that approximately 5.8 million students were enrolled in higher education. There is fierce competition to gain entry into the best public universities, particularly to study subjects such as medicine, law, and engineering.

Between November and January, thousands of 18-year-olds crowd into lecture halls, gymnasiums, and even soccer stadiums to take the *vestibular* (vehs-tee-boo-LAHR), a university entrance examination that Brazilian universities use to select their students. It is common for students from affluent families to pay for expensive courses or to attend private schools that will prepare them better for these demanding university entrance examinations. To ensure that everyone gets an equal opportunity, the government offers tax relief to certain private higher-education institutions for admitting students from poorer backgrounds.

The 15th birthday is a milestone in the life of any Brazilian girl. From then on, she is no longer treated as a girl but as a woman.

INTERNET LINKS

www.brasil.gov.br/

This portal of the government of Brazil provides up-to-date news and information on topics of education, health, economy, citizenship, sports, and more.

www.nationmaster.com/country/br-brazil/lif-lifestyle

This website contains a vast compilation of facts, figures, statistics, and information on a wide variety of Brazil's lifestyle categories, including happiness and life-satisfaction levels.

http://genderindex.org/country/brazil

This website for the Social Institutions and Gender Index provides expert analysis and statistics about gender equality in Brazil, covering issues such as ownership rights and civil liberties.

www.everyculture.com/Bo-Co/Brazil.html

This website provides general information on the traditions, customs, culture, etiquette, social stratifications, and lifestyles of Brazilians.

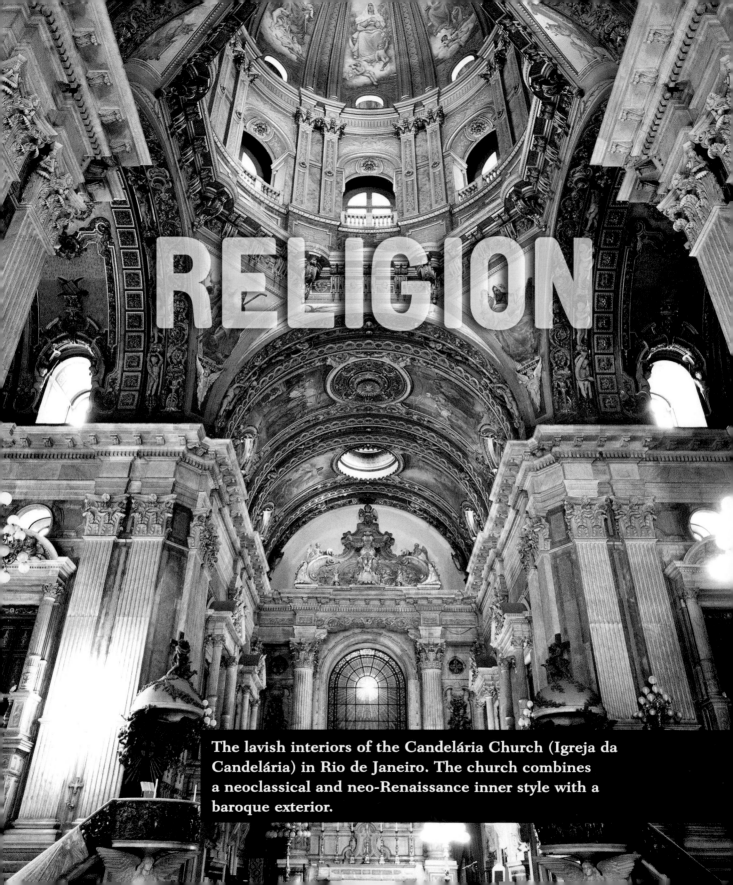

RELIGION

The lavish interiors of the Candelária Church (Igreja da Candelária) in Rio de Janeiro. The church combines a neoclassical and neo-Renaissance inner style with a baroque exterior.

ALMOST 74 PERCENT OF BRAZILIANS are Roman Catholic, making Brazil the world's largest Catholic nation. However, the Catholicism practiced in Brazil has been strongly influenced by local cultures and beliefs.

According to the 2000 census, 15.4 percent of Brazilians are Protestants, 1.3 percent are Spiritualists, 0.3 percent practice the Bantu or voodoo faiths, 1.8 percent follow other religions, and 7.6 percent profess no or unspecified religions.

On New Year's Eve in Rio de Janeiro, women dressed in white march across the beach and into the sea, carrying a statue of the

The hyperboloid structure of the Cathedral of Brasília was designed by architect Oscar Niemeyer with its glass roof seeming to reach or open toward the heavens.

Wax molds of hands hanging from the ceiling of the Our Lady of Aparecida museum's "hall of promises."

Virgin Mary. They launch miniature boats carrying flowers and perfume. If the boats make it out to sea, it means their offerings have been accepted. If they wash to shore, then they have been rejected.

On the third Thursday of January in Salvador da Bahia, women dressed in colorful clothing scrub the steps leading to the Church of Nosso Senhor do Bonfim. In the "miracle room" of this church, hundreds of wax models of human limbs are displayed as tokens of thanks by the faithful who believe they were healed by Nosso Senhor do Bonfim, or Our Lord of the Good Ending.

In October in Belém, thousands join a procession leading a statue of Our Lady of Nazareth through the city streets. They hold on to a thick rope, several blocks long, which is used to pull the carriage bearing the statue. They believe that Our Lady of Nazareth will answer their prayers for helping her along the streets.

The same month, in Rio de Janeiro, thousands of faithful get down on their knees and climb the 365 steps leading up to the Church of Our Lady of the Cliff. They do this to atone for their sins or to express gratitude for favors received.

FOLK RELIGION

The ceremonies Brazilian Catholics celebrate show the influence of African and, to a lesser extent, indigenous Indian religions. The New Year's Eve festival is dedicated to Iemanjá, the African goddess of the sea. Missionaries started Belém's annual procession in 1763 as a way to attract Amazon Indians to Christianity.

Catholic priests arrived in Brazil with the early colonizers and set out to convert the Indians and, later, the African slaves. They achieved partial success: Their pupils became Catholics in name, but they molded their new religion to fit old spiritual practices. The missionaries could do little about this because of their small numbers. To this day, Brazil suffers from a shortage of priests.

The shortage of priests has acutely influenced the religious practices of the poor. Left to their own devices, the poor developed their own form of folk Catholicism. They adopted some elements of Indian religions, such as asking medicine men to heal sicknesses. Of all the non-Christian religions, the African ones were the most influential. Brazilians took on African gods called *orixás* (oh-ree-SHAHS) and gave them Christian names. Oxala came to be represented by Jesus Christ, popularly known as Nosso Senhor do Bonfim. Ogun, a hunter god, and Xango, a god of lightning, took on the identities of saints Anthony and George. Iemanjá, as we have seen, is portrayed as the Virgin Mary. Saints Jerome, Cosmos, Damian, Barbara, Anna, and many others inherited the identities of African *orixás*.

Some worshipers believe that saints are almost as important as the Virgin Mary or Jesus Christ. To many, the main concern is not salvation or life after death so much as surviving in this world. They pray to the saints, who they believe are capable of bestowing favors upon those who revere them. Saint Anthony, for example, is believed to help single women find husbands, Saint Blase protects against sore throats, and Saint Lucia is the patron saint of the blind.

To win a saint's favor, believers make promises. They may promise to climb the steps of a church on their knees or to wash the church. If a saint cures them of an affliction, they may make a pilgrimage to the saint's shrine to offer a model of their healed limb or organ. In larger cities, processions honoring various saints are common. Every town organizes a procession on the feast day of its patron saint. One survey showed that the Brazilian Catholic Church organizes more than 37,000 processions annually—more than 100 each day!

Catholic faithful carry a statue of the Virgin Mary in Brazil's northeast.

THE CHURCH'S SOCIAL ROLE

While they have always been few in number, Catholic priests have played an important role throughout Brazil's history in working for the well-being of the masses.

Jesuit priests arrived with the earliest colonizers and provided education for the settlers and the Indians. They also fought vigorously to protect the Indians from slavery, until their efforts caused the Portuguese king to expel them from Brazil in 1759.

During the colonial period, priests began to establish lay brotherhoods, some of which still exist today. These organizations played the role of a social-security agency. They provided help for elderly or sick members and built numerous hospitals, orphanages, and churches.

Today Brazilian priests have taken a leading role in pushing for aid to indigenous Indians, landless peasants, and the poor. The National Council of Brazilian Bishops has said that the Church should not support political parties but should strive to promote the fair use of land and the fair treatment of workers.

Radical priests accept the doctrine of liberation theology, which combines Marxism and Christianity. They believe that a struggle by the poor working class is needed to carry out God's plan. Liberation theology shows the extremes to which some priests have taken their role as agents of social change.

Nowadays it is impossible to distinguish between traditional Catholics and folk Catholics. Many Brazilian Catholics accept some folk beliefs. In general, however, the difference follows economic lines: The upper class adheres to traditional Catholic beliefs more than the poor do, with the middle class somewhere in between.

AFRICAN RELIGIONS

African rituals still thrive in Brazil, particularly among the poor. Usually carried out at night in special ceremonial houses, they play a part in preserving Afro-Brazilian heritage. The priest or priestess who directs these rites can often tell the story of his or her ancestors going back to when they left Africa in slave ships. However, these African religions have been influenced by European and Indian practices. Many nonblacks have been accepted as members of these cults. Social status rather than ethnicity is the criterion for membership. If active members should earn enough money to rise into the middle or upper classes, their new social position would probably force them to quit.

Religions introduced from West Africa are the roots from which most Brazilian rituals evolved. In Africa these cults centered around the ceremonial preparation of an object known as a fetish, which supposedly held supernatural powers. In Brazil the fetish has given way to the powers of the *orixás*.

Candomblé (kahn-dohm-BLEH) and macumba, the two main cults, reflect the varying degrees of outside influence on African religions. *Candomblé*, practiced mainly in Salvador da Bahia, has stayed closer to its West African roots. Macumba, practiced mostly in Rio de Janeiro, brings beliefs from West and South Africa together with European beliefs.

CANDOMBLÉ A *pai de santo* (pah-ee deh SAHN-teh), or father of the saint, or *mai de santo* (mah-ee deh SAHN-teh), or mother of the saint, presides over a *candomblé* ritual; both men and women are allowed to serve. The inner circle of devotees are the *filhos de santo* (FEE-loos deh SAHN-teh), or children of the saint. In Bahia, these young women usually undergo a complicated initiation ritual to reach this stage.

African slaves in Brazil were forced by their Catholic masters to give up their African religions. Instead of abandoning their gods completely, the slaves just gave the African gods Christian names. Iemanjá, the goddess of rivers and water, came to be represented by the Virgin Mary, the queen of the heavens and seas. Oxala, the most powerful African god and the god of fertility and harvests, came to be represented by Jesus Christ. Exu, a wicked spirit, came to be represented by Satan.

Candomblé priests and priestesses preside over a ceremony. Leading *candomblé* priestesses are said to be able to tell the names of their ancestors as far back as when their ancestors were still in Africa. Before these priestesses die, they pass on their knowledge to their understudies, who will memorize by heart the entire family tree.

For a period of up to one year, the *filhos de santo* must remain inside the ceremonial house of their *pai de santo*, eating a set diet and observing a strict set of rules. When this is completed, they are bathed in water spiced with scented leaves, after which the blood of a sacrificed animal is poured over their heads.

The main *candomblé* ritual is the giving of a meal to the *orixás*. On set dates, the *pai de santo* prepares a fetish for a designated god. The fetish for each *orixá* must be prepared differently. For Xango, whose fetish is a stone, he will place the stone in a basin, surround it with palm oil and sacred leaves, and then spill the blood of a sacrificed rooster over it. The *pai de santo* places the fetish in a special worship room. Followers crowd around the room, with one side reserved for a band of drummers. The *pai de santo* stands in the center, surrounded by the *filhos de santo*.

Several small initial offerings are made to different *orixás*, always starting with the evil spirit named Exu. It is believed that an early gift to this god prevents his interference in later offerings.

Accompanied by the thumping of the drums, the *filhos de santo* dance and sing invocations to different *orixás*. Hours pass, the rhythm of the drumbeat gets faster, the dancing becomes more frenzied, and emotions build up. The climax comes when an *orixá* possesses the spirit of one of the dancers. The entranced *filho de santo* begins to shake uncontrollably until she collapses. When she revives, the *pai de santo* gives her the symbol of the *orixá* who visited her soul, and she continues to dance. Those present revere the *orixá* in her and ask favors of it. During the ceremony, which may last all night, several *orixás* will make their presence known.

MACUMBA Followers of macumba appeal to a wider array of spirits. This cult combines elements of *candomblé* with the ancestral worship brought to Brazil by slaves from the south of Africa and with the European philosophy of spiritualism. According to this philosophy, the living can communicate with the souls of the dead.

The macumba and *candomblé* rites are similar, but the spirits that possess macumba dancers are not always *orixás*. It is believed they may represent a natural force, a god, or an ancestor of one of the followers. The spirits sometimes speak to those present through the voice of the possessed *filho de santo.* Just as often, it is believed, fun-loving spirits just want to use their hosts as the means to drink, dance, smoke, and have a good time. Special macumba ceremonies focus solely on healing. In these, only the *pai de santo* becomes entranced. Possessed by the appropriate spirit, he is believed to be able to cure afflictions simply by blowing cigar smoke over his patient or brushing feathers over the wounded area.

A *candomblé* priest, or *pai de santo*, arranges African and Catholic items on his home altar.

RURAL MIRACLE WORKERS

A different type of religion flourishes in the harsh conditions of Brazil's northeast. Dry weather makes life difficult for the farmers in this region, so they are understandably drawn to preachers who herald the end of this world and the beginning of a new, more just society.

Over the years, many such ministers have won the reputation of being miracle workers. Two of the most famous ones, Antônio Conselheiro and Father Cicero, drew large numbers of followers in the late 19th century. Even today, these rural miracle workers in the northeast are revered as saints.

ANTÔNIO CONSELHEIRO Antônio Maciel, who became known as Antônio Conselheiro, or Antônio the Counselor, began preaching in 1873. He believed that the world would come to an end by 1899, when King Sebastian would appear in Brazil to bring justice to all. This 16th-century Portuguese king had disappeared during a Holy Crusade to North Africa, and many people at that time regarded him as a savior who would reappear to end injustice.

A sculpture of Padre Cicero in a church in Brazil.

Conselheiro gained a reputation as a miracle worker and soon found himself thronged by followers. He also found himself in trouble when the army overthrew Dom Pedro II in 1889.

Brazil's new government did not like him, since he had always taught those who listened to him that an emperor ruled by divine right. The army sent four expeditions against New Jerusalem, the city Conselheiro had built in Bahia as his base. The first three failed, but the fourth, in 1897, destroyed the town and its leader. According to legend, only a child, an old man, and two wounded men survived. The world did end for Conselheiro and his followers, but myths about him live on in the northeast today.

FATHER CICERO A contemporary of Conselheiro, Father Cicero, a priest from the state of Ceará, fared better. He lives on after death as a religious icon and an object of worship.

He first became popular because of his compassion for the poor. However, he became famous in 1890 because of the "miracle of the host." During a Mass that year, a woman who received Holy Communion from him immediately collapsed to the floor with blood dripping from her mouth. Believers claimed the host had physically turned into the flesh and blood of Jesus Christ.

Skeptics claimed that sickness made the woman cough up blood, so the local bishop sent in investigators. His team concluded that no miracle had taken place, and the Church eventually excommunicated Father Cicero, but this did not hurt his popularity.

The people of the northeast believed the priest had magical powers. They saved everything he touched, from his clipped fingernails to the water he used to wash his clothes. When Father Cicero died in 1934, he was one of the most influential men in Brazil.

He is still revered today. A 75-feet (23-m) statue of him stands in the town of Juazeiro do Norte, where thousands arrive each year to visit his grave. Shops all over the northeast sell images of Father Cicero, and many

Brazilians pray to him for favors. Some people believe he has not died but will return soon to herald the coming of a new age.

EVANGELICALS

It is estimated that in 2010, about 20 percent of the population, or 40 million Brazilians, were Evangelical Protestants, with the majority members of the Assemblies of God.

Evangelical churches are now exerting a growing influence in Brazilian politics. The 2010 elections were significant, with nearly 20 million Brazilians casting votes for Marina Silva, who is a high-profile member of the Assemblies of God.

Evangelical members of congress are often elected to safeguard and promote the interests of their churches, which also control a large part of the media. It is believed that many evangelicals refused to vote for President Rousseff because of her positions on abortion and homosexuality. The increasing political power of the evangelicals was established after the 2010 election, which resulted in the appointment of 68 federal deputies and three senators, almost double the evangelical representation before the election.

INTERNET LINKS

ww.celebratebrazil.com/brazil-religion.html

This website offers a brief but informative range of religions found in Brazil, along with local beliefs and customs.

http://eyesonbrazil.com/2008/04/24/macumba-black-magic/

This website provides an overview of the history of macumba and its practice in Brazil today.

http://wn.com/Protestantism_in_Brazil

The official website of World News Network provides a film clip on the growth of the Protestant religion in Brazil.

LANGUAGE

Most newsstand items in Brazil are printed in Portuguese.

9

Portuguese is spoken by nearly 100 percent of the population, uniting the people of Brazil.

BRAZIL IS THE ONLY LATIN American country where the national language is Portuguese. Like other countries of North and South America, Brazil inherited its language from European colonizers.

BRAZILIAN PORTUGUESE

As the English spoken in the United States differs in some ways from that spoken in England, so has Brazil's Portuguese developed a character of its own. Educated citizens of Brazil and Portugal can still communicate and have a fruitful conversation once they adjust to each other's accents. Working-class Brazilians, however, would have a hard time understanding Portuguese speakers in Europe.

The difference between the two stems mostly from the influence of Brazil's Indians. The early colonists survived by trading with these Indians, so they had to learn to communicate with them. For the first 200 years of Brazil's history, an Indian language called Tupi-Guarani was used more than Portuguese.

Today Tupi-Guarani survives only among a few Indian groups living near the border with Paraguay, but it left its mark on Brazilian Portuguese. One researcher compiled a list of 20,000 Portuguese words with Indian origins, making up about one-sixth of the total Portuguese vocabulary. Portuguese settlers borrowed most Indian words to name unfamiliar animals and plants. Some of the names, such as *manioc* and *jaguar*, have even found their way into the English language.

Other outside influences have flavored Brazil's Portuguese. In Bahia and Rio de Janeiro, Brazilians speak with a flowing, almost musical rhythm. Many attribute this to the African heritage of the states. The vocabulary and cadence in some southern towns, in turn, reflect the influence of German, Italian, and Spanish immigrants. The Portuguese spoken in Portugal is said to be increasingly influenced by the Portuguese's watching of Brazilian telenovelas. However, Portuguese and Brazilian Portuguese are now recognized as separate languages, and there have been changes made in official rules governing Brazilian spelling.

ALPHABETS AND ACCENTS

The Portuguese alphabet has three fewer letters than the English alphabet has. In everyday Brazilian Portuguese conversation, the letters *k*, *w*, and *y* of the English alphabet appear only in personal names and words derived from English.

Young boys reading a book together in Fortaleza, Ceará.

The 23 letters of the Portuguese alphabet are pronounced much the way they are in English, except for the letter *x*, which sounds like "sh." For example, the name *Xingu* is pronounced "Shingu."

As in English, *c* can have a hard or soft sound. When it is annotated with a cedilla, appearing as *ç*, it is pronounced softly. For example, *açucar*, meaning "sugar," is pronounced "ah-SOO-kahr."

Portuguese makes extensive use of accent marks. All five vowels take the acute (´) and grave (`) accents. In addition, *a*, *e*, and *o* sometimes take the circumflex (^). The diaeresis (¨) sometimes appears on *i* and *u*, whereas the tilde (~) is used with *a* and *o*. Unaccented Portuguese words are usually stressed on the starting syllable if they end in *a*, *e*, or *o* sounds. Otherwise the emphasis falls on the final syllable. For example, *casa*, meaning "house," is pronounced "KAH-zah," whereas *casar*, meaning "to marry," is pronounced "kah-ZAHR."

In 2008 Portugal's parliament voted to make important changes to the Portuguese language in order to spell hundreds of words according to the Brazilian way. The changes included the standardization of differences in spellings. In an attempt to make Internet searches more efficient, it also added *k*, *w*, and *y* to the alphabet.

When the Portuguese first arrived in Brazil, they found Indians speaking different languages. Few of these dialects still exist today. If Brazilian children spoke the language of the Kayapo Indians who live in the Xingu National Park, they would count to 10 like this:

1	pudi
2	amaikrut
3	amaikrutikeke
4	amaikrutamaikrut
5	amaikrutamaikrutikeke
6	amaikrutamaikrutamaikrut
7	amaikrutamaikrutamaikrutikeke
8	amaikrutamaikrutamaikrutamaikrut
9	amaikrutamaikrutamaikrutamaikrutikeke
10	amaikrutamaikrutamaikrutamaikrutamaikrut

NAMES

In general, Brazilians are warm and friendly and love good conversation in a cheerful atmosphere. At the same time, they are very aware of the codes of social standing and are careful to show proper respect at all times with people they talk to. The manner in which they address one another reflects both the formal and informal sides of their personalities.

Formal Names Brazilians only use the Portuguese equivalent of "you" when speaking to close friends, children, and those from the lower classes. With senior citizens, casual acquaintances, and strangers, they use *o senhor*, meaning "the gentleman," or *a senhora*, meaning "the lady." Instead of asking "How are you today?" they ask "How is the lady (or gentleman) today?"

TALKING WITH THE HANDS

Brazilians are uninhibited when they talk. Good conversation means loud voices and lots of gestures. From the Brazilian point of view, people who talk with a level voice, keeping their hands by their side, don't really appear to believe what they are saying. Here are a few Brazilian hand gestures.

__Brushing the fingertips__ This is a versatile gesture. You shake your hands back and forth so that the fingertips of one hand brush against those of the other. This usually means, "I don't care" or "It doesn't matter." Asked how he is doing, a bored man may respond with this gesture and a shoulder shrug to indicate that things are as usual, not too good and not too bad.

__Kissing the fingertips__ "Everything's great!" This is shown by holding all five fingers of one hand up to the mouth, kissing them, and then opening up the hand as you fling it forward. This gesture is also used to express appreciation for a beautiful painting or woman.

__Finger snap__ One of the most common gestures is to make a snapping sound with the fingers. Holding thumb and middle finger together, the Brazilian relaxes the hand and shakes it so that the index finger whips against the middle finger. Brazilian children learn this at an early age, but foreigners have a hard time picking it up. Brazilians snap their fingers so often it is impossible to assign a precise meaning to the gesture. They snap their fingers to indicate pain, to tell friends to hurry up, or to show appreciation for a joke. If children disobey their parents, their friends snap their fingers as if to say, "Boy, are you in trouble now!"

Finger under the eye *When an American finds something hard to believe, he or she may exclaim, "In a pig's eye!" Brazilians indicate disbelief by pointing to the eye with a knowing grin and gently pulling down the skin beneath the eye. They may emphasize the point by saying, "Aqui, oh!" (ah-KEE, oh), meaning "Sure, right here!"*

Fingers pointing up *"I can't take it anymore!" Holding the fingers together with hands pointing upward means you have had enough. Brazilians also use this gesture when talking about a crowded place.*

Other gestures *Brazilians show a clenched fist to accuse someone of being a miser without calling the person a* pão duro *(pow DOO-roh), or "hard piece of bread." When Brazilians hold the thumb and index finger together at the mouth and motion drinking from a cup, you know they are saying, "Let's have a drink." To show approval or to indicate that everything is all right, Brazilians give the thumbs-up.*

Brazilians often bestow further honorary titles on wealthier or better-educated citizens. Just because someone is called Colonel da Silva does not necessarily mean he is a military officer. Likewise, Doctor da Silva may not be a physician, just a prosperous merchant who knows how to read and conjugate verbs in the subjunctive tense. This is particularly true in rural towns where many older people are illiterate. Those who can decipher official documents have a place of honor in the community.

Yanomami Indians in an invitation talk. The messenger of the guest party embraces the headman of the host party.

INFORMAL NAMES In general, knowing someone's full name is not as important in Brazil as it is in the United States or Europe. Often introductions will not be made when a Brazilian brings a friend to a party. Doing so adds an air of formality to a friendly setting. If an introduction is made, only the first name or nickname is given.

Another reason for this is that Brazilians often do not know the last name of their friends. Most Brazilians are known by either their first or their last name, but not both. A teacher named Carlos Mattos would be called Professor Carlos by his students and Senhor Carlos by his colleagues. His close friends would simply call him Carlos, but many of those who know him would not know his last name.

Brazilians often use names that do not appear on their birth certificates. Adults often christen young children with nicknames that last a lifetime. Brazil's most famous soccer player, known to his countrymen and to the world as Pelé, is really Edson Arantes do Nascimento. Two top players of Brazil's 1990 FIFA World Cup team go by the names Careca, meaning "bald man," and Alemão, meaning "German." This practice is not limited to sports stars.

Brazilians know Luiz Inácio Lula da Silva, the president of Brazil from 2003 through 2010, as Lula. Brazilian children know the folk story about Lampião, a famous bandit of the northeast. However, few children recognize him by his full name, Virgulino Ferreira. Brazil's most famous sculptor is known as Aleijadinho, which means "The Little Cripple."

BODY LANGUAGE

Actions speak louder than words when Brazilians greet one another. For a business contact or a new acquaintance, a handshake suffices, perhaps with a pat on the back if the setting is informal.

But a meeting of friends calls for something more. Two men exchange an *abraço* (ah-BRAH-soo), a firm hug, whereas women trade *beijinhos* (bay-JIN-hoos), kisses on the cheek. By custom, a married woman receives a kiss on each side of the face, but a single woman gets an extra kiss. If it does not come, she is liable to say, "Give me three so that I won't be an old maid!" When men and women meet, they are slightly more restrained, but relatives and friends still trade one or two *beijinhos*.

As this custom shows, physical contact is more common in Brazil than in the United States. Foreigners often feel uncomfortable about how close Brazilians stand in conversation and about the way they grab or touch the arm to emphasize a point.

Brazilians, in turn, do not understand why Americans do things like excuse themselves when squeezing through a crowd, for example. To Brazilians, brushing by to get out of an elevator or nudging someone to the side with the touch of the hand requires no apology or excuse.

INTERNET LINKS

www.kwintessential.co.uk/country/brazil/portuguese-language-of-brazil.html

This website provides a quick introduction to the main languages and dialects spoken in Brazil.

www.justbrazil.org/brazil/portuguese-language.asp

This website features a summary of languages of Brazil with a focus on the body language and gestures used widely by many Brazilians as a way of communicating.

www.native-languages.org/brazil.htm

This comprehensive website provides information on the Native American tribes and languages of Brazil, with recommended books on Brazilian Indians and their culture.

ARTS

Located in the heart of Manaus inside the Amazon rain forest, the Teatro Amazonas (Amazon Theater) was built in 1896.

10

MORE THAN ANY OTHER ART FORM, Brazil's music best captures the nation's heritage. Brazilian music developed from the blending of European, African, and indigenous Indian roots.

The first Jesuit missionaries in Brazil discovered that ritual chanting accompanied by rattles and panpipes played a key role in the religious rites of the indigenous Indians. These missionaries then taught the Indians the Catholic Mass using Gregorian chants. This Indian tradition still survives in the *caboclinho* (kah-boh-KLEEN-hoo), a folk dance of Brazil's northeast. Dressed in Indian outfits, the entourage marches in two columns. A chief recites passages, finishing each line on a low note, and the other dancers respond with a set chorus. A three-man band accompanies the entourage: one man playing the flute; another the *reco-reco* (HEH-koh HEH-koh), a small percussion instrument; and the third a drum.

The men and women of the Xingu tribe performing a traditional dance.

Brazilian culture is mainly derived from Portuguese culture and shares many of its influences in music, painting, literature, and poetry.

Music and dance also played an essential role in the rites of the African slaves. The early colonists considered the slaves' dances wild and obscene and tried to suppress them. Plantation owners, on the other hand, appreciated the musical skills of their slaves and taught them to play European instruments. Bands of slaves provided the music when owners entertained. Gradually African rhythms and instruments found their way into mainstream music. By the early 1800s, colonial barons and ladies in elegant salons found themselves dancing the *lundu* (loon-DHUH), then still regarded as a primitive, lascivious dance. Today's samba is a direct descendant of the *lundu*.

At the same time, the slaves learned to appreciate European instruments, such as the accordion, the tambourine, and the guitar. These instruments still form the backbone of Brazil's music. The Africans adapted these to their style and incorporated some European rhythms and harmonies.

THE NATIONAL BEAT

Just as European, African, and Indian heritages have mixed to produce countless ethnic variations in Brazil, so have these cultures combined to produce an incredible array of music and dance styles. Of the many categories of music in Brazil, the most famous is the samba.

Samba is the national dance of Brazil and is one of the best-known forms of Afro-Brazilian dances. *Samba do morro* (SAHM-bah duh MOH-hoh), or hill samba, refers to samba music played by a large group using only percussion instruments.

In Carnival parades, the samba schools play *samba de enredo* (ehn-HEH-doh), or samba of the street, with a lead singer and a chorus accompanying the percussion band. Small groups in nightclubs perform *samba canção* (kahn-SAH-oo), or samba song, and *samba de salão* (deh SAH-lah-oo), or parlor samba. To a samba beat, the lead vocalist may croon a romantic song of love or make a sarcastic commentary on local politics. *Samba de roda* (deh ROH-dah), or circle samba, is the traditional slave dance, where participants sit in a circle with only one person dancing in the middle. The dancers take turns in the middle. When they finish their turn, they designate the next dancer by standing in front of that person and thrusting their hips forward.

In a *samba rural* (HOO-rah-oo), also called *samba paulista* (pah-hoo-LEES-tah), dancers line up in two rows, whereas in a *samba lençol* (lehn-SOHL), or sheet samba, couples dance in step.

BUMBA-MEU-BOI

Portuguese colonists brought several dramatic folk dances called *folguedos* (fohl-GAY-doos) to Brazil. Usually performed during religious festivals, many survive to this day. The *congada* (cohng-GAH-deh) reenacts a battle of the Crusades between Christians and Moors, whereas the *cavalhada* (kah-val-LEE-ah-dah) mimics a medieval jousting competition.

The *bumba-meu-boi* (boom-bah may-AH-boy), the most common surviving dance, is uniquely Brazilian. Folk groups around the country perform it during the Christmas season. The dance centers on the death and resurrection of a bull. Some people consider it a parody of a bullfight, whereas others believe its origin lies in the rites of pagan religions that worshiped the bull as a symbol of power and fertility.

The plot usually has a cowboy named Mateus trying to sell a bull to a wealthy rancher. The bull attacks the crowd that surrounds it, is stabbed with a knife, and dies. Mateus, however, revives it using folk medicine.

The *bumba-meu-boi* is now mainly a festive occasion, filled with bright costumes and lively music and dance. Witty exchanges between the soloists and the chorus add elements of humor and social commentary.

The star of the dance is the bull. One man plays the part, bearing on his shoulders a bull-shape wooden framework covered with velvet. Authentic bull's horns, elegant stitching, ribbons, and sometimes even colorful semiprecious stones decorate the cloth.

Always the center of attention, the bull attacks, then retreats, shudders in the throes of death, then bounces back to life. In the end, it breaks out of the circle of dancers and leads a festive procession through the streets. There are various interpretations of the symbolism of the *bumba-meu-boi*. In essence, it celebrates the concepts of strength, virility, rebirth, and ultimately hope—elements vital to the Brazilian identity.

A dancer dressed as a bull for the *bumba-meu-boi*, a comic representation of Portugal's nonlethal bullfights. This very rhythmic and colorful dance is performed most authentically in the northeastern states of Brazil.

A band made up of children play traditional Brazilian instruments at a local music festival.

MUSICAL INSTRUMENTS

EUROPEAN INSTRUMENTS The Portuguese contributed an array of stringed instruments to Brazil's music. The Portuguese guitar, the *viola* (vee-OH-lah), was the favorite instrument of Iberian musicians as far back as the 13th century. This 10-string instrument is gradually giving way to the modern six-string guitar, but it is still an essential part of Brazilian folk music.

The *cavaquinho* (kah-vah-KEEN-uh), a small guitar similar to a Hawaiian ukelele; the *bandolim* (bahn-doh-LEEM), which is a mandolin; and the *rabeca* (hah-BEH-kah), a Portuguese fiddle, live on as well. Virtuoso performers on these instruments come together to play a lively acoustic style Brazilians call *choro* (SHOH-roh) music, from the Portuguese word meaning "cry" or "lament."

The accordion, the tambourine, and the triangle all came to Brazil from Europe. So did the *tarol* (tah-ROHL) and the *surdo* (SOOR-doh). The *tarol* is a small snare drum similar to those used in marching bands, whereas the *surdo* is a large bass drum.

AFRICAN INSTRUMENTS Brazil inherited numerous instruments from Africa, including the unique *cuica* (koo-EE-kah), which produces a most unusual squeal. A narrow rod fastened to the middle of the drumhead extends through the hollow cylinder of the *cuica*. Musicians rub a damp cloth along this rod. The friction causes the leather skin to vibrate, creating a high-pitched sound, something like the noise a damp cloth makes when rubbed against a window. By pressing their fingers at different points along the drumhead and varying the speed at which they rub the rod, the musicians can control the noise the *cuica* makes.

Another African import is the *tamborim* (tahm-boor-IM), a small drum the size of a tambourine that does not have metallic discs and is not meant to be shaken. Samba masters usually hold it in one hand while drumming it with a small baton.

Another popular instrument is the *reco-reco*, a term used to describe a frog's croak. It is the Brazilian version of the Dominican guiro, or gourd, but made out of bamboo cylinders with grooves—a stick is scraped along the carved notches of the wooden instrument to produce a similar sound.

The *berimbau* (bee-rim-BOW) also makes a unique sound. With one wire tied between the ends of a slightly curved stick, it looks like an archer's bow. Master players twang the wire by hitting it with a stick. They vary the note by using their free hand to tighten or loosen the wire. A gourd attached to the bottom of the *berimbau* acts as a resonator. The musician holds it against his stomach to start, then changes the timbre of the sound by moving it to and from his body. The *berimbau* is today used exclusively to accompany *capoeira* (cah-poh-EE-rah), an African martial-arts dance featuring exotic leaps and kicks.

INDIAN INSTRUMENTS Rattles and pipes are the preferred instruments of Brazil's Indians. Some Indian groups in the Amazon still bring out the *urua* (OO-roo-ah) for formal ceremonies. It takes a barrel-chested Indian with above-average lung capacity to blow music out of this 10-feet-long (3-m-long) pipe. Simpler and more common is the *pife* (peef), a bamboo flute still popular among the poor in the north and the northeast. The standard Indian rattle is the maraca, a hollow gourd with a wooden handle partially filled with dried seeds. Africans also brought rattles with them to the New World, so scholars can only guess the origin of the several varieties used in Brazil.

One cliché is that Brazil is a country of rhythm. What it really has are many rhythms. Brazil is still one of the best places in the world for grassroots ethnic music.

POPULAR ART

Popular art flourishes in open-air markets called *feiras* (FAY-rahs). In the rural towns of the interior, the *feiras* are big events. Vendors sell everything from chickens to pots and pans to carved nativity sets to cotton clothing. In larger cities, the *feiras* focus more on popular art than on daily essentials.

Good-luck charms are best-sellers at the *feiras*. Tiny fruit and animal figures created by silversmiths in Bahia are said to represent *candomblé* spirits. People wear a *balangandã* (bah-lahng-gahn-DAH), a cluster of such figures on a chain, believing it has the power to ward off evil spirits.

Another charm is the *figa* (FEE-gah), a model of a clenched fist where the thumb sticks out between the index and middle fingers. It was brought to Brazil by Africans in the 16th century. Many Brazilians wear it to fend off the "evil eye." Artisans usually sell these charms in all sizes, made from wood, silver, or semiprecious stones.

Many artists run shops near churches dedicated to popular saints. They specialize in creating *ex votos* (ehs VOH-toos), a product of rural art and Catholicism and a unique form of popular art. These are the items that Catholics offer to saints as payment for favors granted. Such an item could be a clay model of a broken leg that is healing or an elaborate painting of a saint's miraculous intercession in a car crash.

Along the São Francisco River, sculptors carve *carrancas* (kah-HAN-kahs), half-human, half-beast creatures, with glaring eyes and sharp teeth.

The *carranca*, a figurehead on boats on the São Francisco River. The river is said to have a history of evil spirits, including Water Monster and Backwoodsman of the Water, who have sunk many ships in the past. The *carranca* is there to scare these monsters away.

LITERATURE

Brazilian literature accounts for half of all literary publications in Latin America. Brazil's postindependence literature described the country's forests, the Indians, the African slaves, and urban activities. The best-known poets of this period included Gonçalves Dias (1823—64), Castro Alves (1847—71), and José de Alencar (1829—77).

Joaquim Maria Machado de Assis (1839—1908) is considered by many to be one of the greatest writers in Brazil and the world, although he did not gain much recognition for his work outside the country. Interestingly, American literary critic Harold Bloom categorizes him as the greatest black writer in Western literature. His literary style is admired for its antirealist elements, which have inspired numerous other writers in Brazil and beyond.

The novels of Joaquim Manuel de Macedo (1820—82) and Alfredo d'Escragnolle Taunay (1843—99) are still widely read in Brazil. José Américo de Almeida (1887—1969) and Jorge Amado (1912—2001) wrote about the problems of life in the northeast. Amado wrote his first novels about cocoa-plantation workers in Bahia and fishermen in coastal villages. These works have been translated into 33 languages. In the 1950s Amado wrote several internationally acclaimed novels.

Brazil's most innovative writer was perhaps João Guimarães Rosa (1908—67). He has been credited with creating through his novels a new style of writing, almost a new language. Contemporary Brazilian authors include Clarice Lispector, Rubem Fonseca, Sérgio Sant'Anna, João Gilberto Noll, Milton Hatoum, Bernardo Carvalho, João Almino, Adriana Lisboa, and Cristovão Tezza. Brazilian poet Ferreira Gullar was recently nominated for the Nobel Prize.

The interior of the Real Gabinete Português de Leitura (Royal Portuguese Reading Room) in Rio de Janeiro. Open to the public since 1900, the library of the Real Gabinete holds the largest collection of Portuguese works outside Portugal.

A representation
of the Last
Supper by artist
Aleijadinho at the
church Bom Jesus
de Matosinhos in
Minas Gerais.

"THE LITTLE CRIPPLE"

Brazil's most famous sculptor, Antônio Francisco Lisboa (1738—1814), is also one of the world's most remarkable artists. Later he became known as Aleijadinho, "The Little Cripple."

Aleijadinho was struck by an unconfirmed disease—perhaps leprosy or arthritis—in the prime of his life. The disease paralyzed his hands but not his passion and determination. He tied a hammer and a chisel to his wrists and continued to work.

Aleijadinho amazingly managed to complete 12 remarkable life-sized soapstone statues of Old Testament prophets and the 66 wood carvings that make up the Stations of the Cross in the town of Congonhas do Campo near Belo Horizonte.

The illegitimate son of a Portuguese architect and a slave, Aleijadinho received no formal education during his 80 years. Yet his masterpieces are considered among the finest of baroque art anywhere in the world. He learned about the European baroque style from books and missionaries.

Along with his sculptures, Aleijadinho designed many beautiful churches, each with trademark large, rounded bell towers, altars featuring ornate engravings, and reliefs of angels and saints extending out of ceilings. Several of these churches stand in various cities throughout the state of Minas Gerais. Two examples are Our Lady of Mount Carmel Church and the São Francisco Chapel. These two churches represent the best of baroque art in Brazil and are considered among the world's finest. Both of them are found in

PAULO COELHO

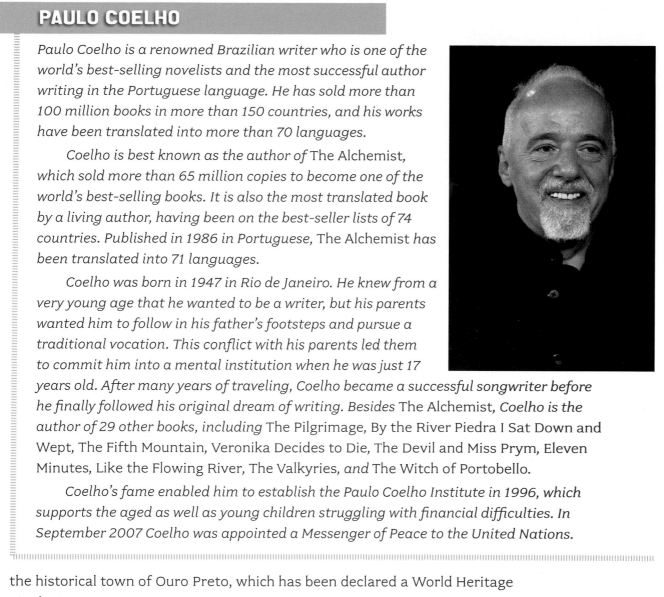

Paulo Coelho is a renowned Brazilian writer who is one of the world's best-selling novelists and the most successful author writing in the Portuguese language. He has sold more than 100 million books in more than 150 countries, and his works have been translated into more than 70 languages.

Coelho is best known as the author of The Alchemist, *which sold more than 65 million copies to become one of the world's best-selling books. It is also the most translated book by a living author, having been on the best-seller lists of 74 countries. Published in 1986 in Portuguese,* The Alchemist *has been translated into 71 languages.*

Coelho was born in 1947 in Rio de Janeiro. He knew from a very young age that he wanted to be a writer, but his parents wanted him to follow in his father's footsteps and pursue a traditional vocation. This conflict with his parents led them to commit him into a mental institution when he was just 17 years old. After many years of traveling, Coelho became a successful songwriter before he finally followed his original dream of writing. Besides The Alchemist, *Coelho is the author of 29 other books, including* The Pilgrimage, By the River Piedra I Sat Down and Wept, The Fifth Mountain, Veronika Decides to Die, The Devil and Miss Prym, Eleven Minutes, Like the Flowing River, The Valkyries, *and* The Witch of Portobello.

Coelho's fame enabled him to establish the Paulo Coelho Institute in 1996, which supports the aged as well as young children struggling with financial difficulties. In September 2007 Coelho was appointed a Messenger of Peace to the United Nations.

the historical town of Ouro Preto, which has been declared a World Heritage Site by UNESCO.

Two blocks from the São Francisco Chapel is the town's monument to Aleijadinho, with his remains buried beneath a marker in a museum church. Some of his wood and soapstone carvings, documents about his career, and the illustrated Bibles he used to study are also displayed in the galleries of the church.

BRASÍLIA'S ARCHITECTURE

Brasília, a planned city built from scratch to be Brazil's capital, was designated a World Heritage Site as well as awarded the status of Historical and Cultural Heritage of Humanity by UNESCO in 1987.

Just as Aleijadinho became a driving force behind the baroque architecture of the town of Ouro Preto, so another famous Brazilian architect is the mastermind of many of the modern ideas seen in the buildings of Brasília.

Oscar Niemeyer has designed numerous buildings in France, Algeria, and the United States as well as all over Brazil. In Brasília he teamed up with noted city planner Lucio Costa and artist Roberto Burle Marx to create his most famous works.

One word sums up Niemeyer's style: simplicity. Never curve a wall when a flat wall will do. Never use bright paints or bricks when the natural color of marble or concrete will be more effective.

The three principal government buildings that border Brasília's Plaza of the Three Powers exhibit Niemeyer's practical design. The twin towers of the National Congress dominate the square, with a concrete dome alongside one tower offsetting an inverted concrete dome next to the other. The president's Palácio do Planalto and the Supreme Court flank the congressional building. Both are similar in design. A long walkway leads up to a large patio, which surrounds a square structure with glass facades on all sides.

Eight pairs of identical government ministry buildings line an esplanade leading up to the Plaza of the Three Powers. The closest ministry to the plaza, however, has its own unique design. Called the Itamaraty Palace, the home of the Foreign Ministry is a glass box encased in a concrete cage sitting in the middle of a pool of water.

The structures may look stark, but when the red evening sun reflects off the glass of the Palácio do Planalto or the waters around the Itamaraty Palace, Brasília takes on a unique beauty.

The outline of Niemeyer's buildings against the bright sky of Brazil's Central Plateau reminds the people of the ultimate symbolism of this planned capital: an expression of their nation's desire to conquer its isolated interior regions.

Niemeyer continues to be Brazil's premier architect. His most recent contribution is the famed Sambódromo, Rio's Carnival grandstand.

Oscar Niemeyer is often referred to as a "sculptor of monuments." His signature buildings are curvy and spacious with exposed spaces and unconventional patterns.

INTERNET LINKS

www.artcyclopedia.com/nationalities/Brazilian.html

This website provides a list of great Brazilian artists and an index of where their art can be viewed at museums worldwide.

www.thecoolist.com/brazilian-architecture-10-breathtaking-modern-monuments/

This comprehensive site provides information about the 10 best modern monuments in Brazil today.

www.brazilianmusic.com/

This website is a source about Brazil's music, culture, and style including articles, interviews, and links to Web sites of many Brazilian artists.

LEISURE

Crowds of people enjoy a relaxing Sunday afternoon at Embaré beach in Santos.

BRAZILIANS LOVE SPORTS. THERE are 8,000 sports clubs throughout the country. The long coastline encourages water sports, such as surfing. Basketball and volleyball are played in some schools and clubs although many schools in the poorer areas may not have adequate sports equipment or facilities. Brazil won the World Basketball Championship twice, in 1959 and 1963. Tennis, boxing, and chess are also popular.

11

Brazil calls itself the "country of football," more widely known as soccer in the United States. The 2014 FIFA World Cup will be hosted by Brazil.

Men enjoying a game of dominoes on a beach in Maranhão.

SOCCER IS KING

Brazilians joke that they save Sunday for two religious ceremonies: They go to church, and then they go to a soccer match.

No sport in Brazil rivals soccer for the sheer enthusiasm of its fans. Brazilian athletes have won medals in sports ranging from swimming to volleyball to track-and-field. But any time you see Brazilian children playing on an open patch of ground, odds are they will be kicking a soccer ball. Scoring a goal in a world soccer championship is the dream of every Brazilian boy.

Brazilians call soccer *futebol* or *futbol* (FOOT-ball), the Portuguese spelling of the English word "football." Soccer came to Brazil from England about a hundred years ago. Most people would agree that Brazilians not only improved the game but also perfected it.

The Brazilian style of play, with its superb dribbling, flamboyant showmanship, graceful playmaking, and incredible goals, continues to delight the world. To Brazilians, the result of a match is not the only thing that matters; the way goals are scored is just as important. Time after time, Brazil seems to be able to pick superb players from out of nowhere and make them the envy of the world. Brazil is the only nation that has played in all 19 FIFA World Cup tournaments, and in 2002 it became the only country to win the competition five times.

Young boys playing soccer in Brasília.

SOCCER PASSION   Soccer enthusiasts around the world consider Brazil's most famous star, Pelé, to be the greatest player of all time. A member of three of Brazil's world championship teams, Pelé scored more than 1,200 goals in national and international competitions in his 18-year career. During the 1970 FIFA World Cup in Mexico, Pelé and other legends such as Tostao, Rivelino, Gerson, and Jairzinho formed a championship team most experts agree was the greatest in history. Today Brazil's soccer heroes include Rivaldo, Ronaldinho, and Kaká, who all play on the national team. Apart from these soccer legends, more than 10,000 Brazilians play soccer professionally across the world.

Brazilians supporting their country's national team at the 2010 FIFA World Cup.

When Brazil's national team plays, the nation comes to a halt. Work stops, traffic disappears from the streets, and even the beaches are deserted. Every television network broadcasts the match, along with several radio networks. Radio announcers break into the familiar extended cry of "gooooooooaaaaaal" when Brazil scores. Fireworks erupt across the skies and people pour into the streets to celebrate victory.

On a smaller scale, this same enthusiasm accompanies matches played almost every day all over the country. There are countless leagues for children, teenagers, and adults. Besides the regular game played on a grass field with 11 players to each side, Brazilians play beach soccer, also known as *beasal* (BEE-sal), on the sand with seven players to each side as well as indoor soccer on a hard surface with six players to each side. There is even a league that plays "car soccer." The players drive cars on an oversize field, pushing a huge balloonlike ball around.

THE FLA-FLU RIVALRY   Rivalries are common in soccer, but few rivalries in the world can match the intensity of clashes between Rio de Janeiro's super clubs, Flamengo and Fluminense. Brazilians refer to these matches as "Fla-Flu" or "Flu-Fla."

Fluminense fans support their team during the Fluminense FC vs. CR Vasco da Gama Futebol Brasileirao League match at the Maracanã Stadium.

Fans assemble throughout the city the morning of the game. Dressed in their team's colors and carrying team flags, they dance and sing from the moment they gather. As the afternoon progresses, thousands of chanting supporters converge on Rio's mammoth Maracanã Stadium, which can seat 95,000 attendees. The red-and-black shirts of Flamengo fans color one side of the stadium, while the red, white, and green of Fluminense dominate the other.

By the time the teams take to the field in the late afternoon, the samba beat has already whipped the fans into a frenzy. They greet the players with an explosion of fireworks and a sea of waving flags. Flamengo fans throw confetti, whereas Fluminense supporters heave talcum powder into the air. All eyes are focused on the field when the game begins. Like a wave, noise rises and falls from one end of the stadium to the other, as the teams take turns dictating the play. The wave of noise crests when a goal is scored. Players on the field and fans in the stands leap into the air and exchange hugs. The flags and fireworks reappear.

At the end of the game, the losing team's supporters fold up their flags, put away their drumsticks, and head home in sorrow. The winners take their party to the streets, hang their flags out of windows, honk car horns, and keep the samba beat going throughout the night. Radio stations will replay narratives of the goals. Monday newspapers will offer diagrams depicting how each goal was scored, along with commentaries on the performance of each player, coach, and referee. Talk of the game goes on everywhere, until the next Sunday's feature match.

A memorable match played between the two rivals was held in 1995 during the Campeonato Carioca final stage match. A player from Fluminense called Renato Gaúcho won the match for his club by one point, scoring a famous goal with his belly.

BEACH FUN

Most people in Brazil live a short bus ride from the ocean, and the beach is a part of daily life.

Brazilians take great pride in the fact that their beaches are open to all—in many areas of the country, the law prohibits private ownership of any part of the beach. Some sociologists even attribute the relative lack of tension between Brazil's social classes to the "democracy" of the beach. When a man is on the beach in his bathing suit, you do not know if he is upper or lower class. The conclusion is that as long as the poor can mingle freely with the wealthy on the beach, they do not feel oppressed.

A man practices *capoeira* at a beach in Brazil. Capoeira is a martial arts dance first introduced by the slaves. Told by their masters to stop, the slaves disguised this foot-fighting technique as a dance, thereby preserving the cultural art form.

In practice, however, groups with different interests each congregate on their own stretch of the beach, informally dividing the sand into little communities. On any beach in Rio de Janeiro, artists and intellectuals frequent one area, members of a political party regularly meet in another. Families with small children stay in one place, teenagers hang around another. The best surfers convene on one stretch, the best volleyball games are found elsewhere. The regulars on the different patches of beach get to know one another. Making a trip to the beach is an opportunity to catch up with the latest news and gossip.

Early in the morning, people go to the beaches to exercise. Lifeguards lead group calisthenic sessions, but the favorite form of exercise is the Cooper Test, a 2.5-mile (4-km) run named after an American doctor who was one of the early advocates of jogging. Running or jogging in Brazil is called "coopering" or "doing the cooper." Signs along the beaches in many cities mark out the distances, and runners crowd the sidewalks in the early morning and late afternoon.

Ipanema and Copacabana in Rio de Janeiro are two of Brazil's best-known beaches. However, with 4,655 miles (7,491 km) of coastline, Brazil has thousands of other beautiful and more remote beaches all over the country.

A VIEW FROM THE SAND

When the sun gets higher in the sky, sunbathers begin to arrive. During the week, many Brazilians take a quick trip to the beach during lunch breaks.

On a sunny weekend, Brazilians cram the beaches by the thousands. Most of them lie on the sand and relax, but it is hardly a quiet atmosphere. Vendors march up and down selling sweets, fruit juices, hot coffee, a local type of tea called maté, soft drinks, ice cream, hot dogs, and an impressive array of beach knickknacks.

Games are played everywhere. Beach-soccer and volleyball boundaries are marked off, complete with makeshift goalposts and nets. Children fly bird-shape kites. Other beachgoers hit rubber balls back and forth using paddles or swat a *peteca* (pay-TAY-kah), a device consisting of long feathers weighted by a bundle of sand wrapped in leather, with their hands.

Before going home, beachgoers stop at one of the open-air cafés along the beach for a drink or a quick bite.

Beachgoers watching the fireworks on New Year's Day from the famed Copacabana beach.

Gradually the afternoon crowd gives way to the night crowd. Couples stroll along the sand holding hands. The boardwalk in many cities becomes an outdoor arts fair, with artisans selling goods from paintings to woven hammocks. Music and conversation continue in the open-air cafés until late at night.

DANCE MUSIC

While for most of the year samba never strays far from their thoughts, during Carnival, samba is all Brazilians have on their mind. Any time a group of Brazilians get together, be it on the beach, on a bus, at a restaurant, or in a soccer stadium, if there is a can to tap or a box of matches to shake, a samba beat is likely to start.

Music and passion are always in fashion when it comes to Brazil's famous beaches.

A group of Brazilian researchers in the Antarctica said they survived the unfamiliar freezing temperatures by warming up with a daily improvised samba session.

When they are not making their own music, Brazilians love to dance to music played by others. Even in small farming communities of the southern and northeastern interior, you can count on finding somewhere to dance any night.

MUSIC FEVER

In a major city like Rio de Janeiro, the options for samba are staggering. The large samba schools raise money and practice for the annual Carnival parade by holding samba parties at their headquarters all year round. These performances draw huge crowds, but smaller bands play samba music in a cozier atmosphere in many nightclubs around town.

Brazil's popular soap opera veterans Claudia Jimenez and Priscila Fantin record an episode of the soap opera *Sete Pecados* in Rio de Janeiro.

String bands playing *choro* (meaning "cry" or "lament") music provide lively music to dance to or simply for listening. Another option is the *gafieira* (gah-fee-AY-rah), a dance hall where Brazilian-style ballroom dancing is practiced. The *maxixe* (mah-SHIH-shih), a favorite dance, combines the rapid rhythms of African and Latin music with the steps of a European polka. Watching the couples swirl around the floor can make spectators dizzy.

Some clubs feature *frevo* (FRAY-voh) dancing, a style Brazilians in the northeast prefer over samba during Carnival. Lovers of music from the northeast can choose other nightspots where *forró* (FOH-hoh) bands perform. The accordion is the main instrument for this kind of music, the favorite of the *sertão* region. Urban Brazilians sometimes joke about *forró* music, much the way some Americans joke about types of country music.

Brazilians musicians have also established their own type of dance music derived from hip-hop and rap music. One of the more popular forms is *funk carioca*, which is a type of dance music from Rio de Janeiro.

As if homegrown music were not enough, Brazilians also love imported music. Dance and music enthusiasts pack discos, rock-and-roll halls, and jazz clubs.

TELEVISION SOAPS

Television in Brazil has historically been managed by the private sector. TV Brasil, the first national public television network, was launched in 2007 to coincide with the launch of digital television in certain major cities, including Brasília, Rio de Janeiro, Salvador, São Luís, and São Paulo.

Television has joined music, soccer, and the beach as a cornerstone of Brazilian leisure activity. Rede Globo, Brazil's largest television network, is the third largest in the world. Only two of the principal U.S. networks—CBS and NBC—operate more stations. Smaller networks also operate in Brazil.

Most of the shows on the air are made in Brazil. The most popular are the telenovelas, long-running serials aired during prime time. These programs can be watched every night, but Rede Globo's feature show, the one bringing together the most stars and the best production team, comes on the air every weeknight at 9:00. These programs are extremely influential; they introduce slang and expressions into Brazilian discourse and trends into Brazilian fashion.

Although they portray Brazilian characters in Brazilian settings, Rede Globo's serials have become hits all over the world. They have been dubbed, for example, in Italian for viewers in Italy and even in Chinese for countries with a large Chinese-speaking viewership.

Although television remains a popular pastime in Brazil, other leisure activities such as browsing the Internet, playing computer games, and watching DVDs are rapidly overtaking television as a major leisure activity.

INTERNET LINKS

www.brasil.gov.br/sobre/sports

The sports section in the official portal of the government of Brazil provides information and the latest news on sporting events, incentive programs, financing, and more.

www.brazilbeaches.org/

The official online guide to Brazil's best beaches provides descriptions complete with attractions, hotels, and tours.

www.allbrazilianmusic.com/

This website provides access to the largest database of Brazilian music and musicians with reliable biographies, discographies, and audio excerpts of a large range of records.

FESTIVALS

A float at the Rio Carnival. Carnival is deeply rooted in ethnic and religious heritage. Some say the word *carnival* comes from the Italian *carne vale*, which means "farewell to meat," since it marks the last days before Lent. Others say it is derived from the Latin *carrum novalis*, the Roman festival float.

12

É *CARNAVAL*! IT'S CARNIVAL TIME! Every year this cry fills the air to start a four-day national holiday. Almost everyone forgets his or her problems, puts on a costume, and dances to the rhythms of samba, *frevo* (FRAY-vuh), and *lambada* (lahm-BAH-deh) music. The celebrations take place in neighborhoods throughout the country.

Brazilians adore music, dancing, and partying. Festive parties are a part of many religious festivals, but the biggest party of all is Carnival. Dating back to early Christian times, this event began as a last chance to feast

Seventy percent of Brazil's tourists visit the country during Carnival to join in the celebrations.

Samba dancers don colorful wigs as they dance at the Rio Carnival parade.

Throngs of crowds gather to watch the wildly decorative festive floats at the Rio Carnival.

before the beginning of Lent. While Carnival is celebrated in countries around the world, no other country's celebration matches the frenzy and excitement of Carnival in Brazil.

Carnival takes place some time in late February or early March. Traditionally it starts the Sunday before Lent and ends on Ash Wednesday, but Brazilians extend the party to a week. During this period, mayors ceremonially hand over the keys of their cities to King Momo, an ancient Greek god of mockery and jest. Many streets are closed to traffic, and thousands throng streets and beaches to sing, dance, and cheer the parades in Brazil's biggest, most colorful party.

CARNIVAL IN RIO DE JANEIRO

The most famous festivities take place in Rio de Janeiro. The biggest event is the parade of the best *escolas de samba* (ess-KOH-lahs deh SAHM-bah), or samba schools, along the Sambódromo stadium. For three nights, thousands of spectators watch the elaborately dressed participants dance and sing their way down the parade route.

NATIONAL HOLIDAYS

January 1	New Year's Day
February/March	Carnival (four days)
March/April	Good Friday and Easter Sunday
April 21	Tiradentes Day (honoring a famous Brazilian revolutionary who fought for Brazilian independence from the Portuguese in the 19th century)
May 1	Labor Day
May/June	Corpus Christi
September 7	Independence Day
October 12	Nossa Senhora de Aparecida Day (honoring the patron saint of Brazil)
November 2	All Souls' Day, also known as Day of the Dead
November 15	Proclamation of the Republic
December 25	Christmas

On Ash Wednesday, an official jury announces its choice for the best school in that year's parade, and the winner's celebration extends the Carnival joy through the weekend.

Dancing is not restricted to the Sambódromo. Merrymakers called *foliões* (foh-lee-OH-ehs) take over the city streets, dressed in clown outfits or swimwear. Groups wearing the same costumes make up a *bloco* (BLOH-koh). The best known is the Bloco das Piranhas, a group of men who take to the streets dressed as women. The *blocos* and *foliões* fall in behind various small samba bands that roam on foot or by car, and spontaneous street parties may erupt anywhere.

Private clubs throw extravagant parties attended by as many as 10,000 people. The most famous is the "Night in Baghdad" theme ball on the last night of Carnival. Partygoers wear either a tuxedo or a costume. In the heat of the crammed ballroom, most opt for the latter.

Samba music and dancing keep the temperature high from midnight until well past breakfast the next morning.

ESCOLAS DE SAMBA

It's Carnival, and one of Rio's best escolas de samba *has filled the mile-long (1.6-km-long) Sambódromo. The school's 3,000 dancers sing and swing to a samba beat pounded out by a 250-member percussion section. Gigantic floats separate groups of dancers dressed in bright costumes. For an hour and a half, this wave of color and sound makes its way along the avenue. The samba schools take turns parading before the huge crowds. Starting at around 8 P.M., they go on until at least 9 A.M. the next morning.*

The schools are actually neighborhood associations, most coming from the poorer areas of the city. All year long, members volunteer their time to put together the extravagant costumes and floats and practice their song and dance routines. Each school's presentation is built around a theme song called samba de enredo. *Through the floats and costumes, they build their theme into a story.*

Generally the theme is Brazilian folklore or history. Occasionally it makes a humorous comment on modern life. In 1990 a group took a theme revolving around a Rio de Janeiro neighborhood known for its sale of stolen property. The percussion section wore police uniforms, whereas some of the costumes and floats portrayed jails, weapons, car tires, and television sets.

The structure of each parade follows a set formula. First comes the abre alas *(are-bray-ARE-las), or opening wing. Accompanied by the first float, this group introduces the main theme. A line of men in dark suits follows. They are the school's figurative board of directors, intended to add an air of dignity to the fun.*

The samba starts in earnest with the arrival of the mestre sala *(mess-tray-SAR-lah) and* porta bandeira *(por-tah-BUN-dee-rah), the school's dance master and flag bearer, respectively. The different wings follow, separated by floats and groups of* passistos *(pah-SEES-toos), the school's most skilled samba dancers, performing elaborate dance steps and acrobatic leaps.*

Each school also features a baiana *wing, in which Afro-Brazilian women in traditional clothing celebrate the African origin of the Brazilian samba. The percussion section, called the* bateria *(bah-teh-REE-ah), starts near the front but goes slower along the avenue for the last group of dancers to catch up so that they can keep up with the beat.*

CARNIVAL IN SALVADOR AND RECIFE

Less vibrant *escola de samba* parades take place in other cities, but the favorite Carnival spots after Rio are in the northeast. The street celebrations in Salvador da Bahia and Recife are almost as intense as Rio's.

Frevo music replaces the samba as the favorite. Based on African rhythms, it originated in Recife. Today the city's expert *frevo* dancers perform in traditional fashion, wearing knee-length pants, long stockings, and baggy shirts and waving bright umbrellas.

The trademark of Salvador's Carnival is a specially equipped truck called the *trio elétrico*. Loudspeakers lining the sides of this truck blast music played by a band on top. The crowds following the truck dance to various types of music, from the traditional *frevo* to the more recent *deboche* (deh-BOHSH) or *lambada*. These newer rhythms draw upon samba, *frevo*, and outside influences such as reggae and rock and roll.

Afoxés (ah-foh-SHEH) also march through the streets of Salvador. Made up of followers of African religions, they sprinkle lavender cologne on the crowd and sing sacred songs, often in African languages.

Recife has neither samba schools nor *trio eletricos,* but there is no shortage of *frevo* bands and costumed *blocos* along its streets. It also has its *maracatu* (mah-rah-kah-TOO) marches, the royal procession of African kings. First practiced by slaves longing for their homeland, the *maracatu* is today reenacted by African groups in Brazil. Other groups wear feathered headdresses and paint their faces to perform the *caboclinho*, a frenetic dance learned from the Indians.

A rural group of Brazilians of African origins conduct a *maracatu* march to the sounds of a percussion band.

RELIGIOUS FESTIVALS

Catholic holy days make up about half of Brazil's national holidays. The feast day of Brazil's patron saint, Nossa Senhora de Aparecida, is unique. In 1717 fishermen in the state of São Paulo found a statue of the Virgin Mary in a river. They built a chapel, and a cult grew around the statue. The chapel

OKTOBERFEST

The biggest festival in the south of Brazil has nothing to do with Africa or the Catholic Church. The Oktoberfest in Blumenau, Santa Catarina, started only in 1982, is now the world's second-largest beer festival. In 2010 more than a half-million people drank more than 128,000 gallons (581,900 l) of beer during the 16-day event. Only the original Oktoberfest in Munich, Germany, exceeds this scale. German immigrants founded Blumenau, and during October there is little evidence of the New World in the city. People listening to the polka bands, eating wurst with sauerkraut, or watching the blonde, blue-eyed women serving beer in the biergarten would be convinced they were in Germany.

Afro-Brazilian worshipers prepare their floral offering to Iemanjá at the Copacabana beach in Rio de Janeiro.

has since become a huge basilica, sitting along the Rio—São Paulo highway. About 8 million devotees visit the church each year, with more than a million during the month of October alone, due to the widespread celebration of Nossa Senhora de Aparecida, Brazil's patron saint day.

Nativity sets and Santa Claus are both part of Christmas in Brazil. Instead of arriving through the chimney, Papai Noel is believed to come in through the window and leave presents in shoes left on the floor. More important than the gift giving is the traditional Christmas Eve dinner, which brings together the entire extended family.

Numerous other religious days are observed across the country. The feast days of saints Anthony (June 12), John (June 23), and Peter (June 28) fall close enough to one another to justify two weeks of partying, called *festas juninas* (FEHS-tahs joo-NEE-nahs). People dress in country style to attend outdoor parties, featuring Brazilian country music and cooking. Fireworks, bonfires, and religious processions are other elements of the festivities. Saint Anthony is the patron saint of single men and women, so staged wedding ceremonies are often played out on his feast day.

Many religious festivals are unique to different regions. New Year's Eve in Rio de Janeiro is the feast day of Iemanjá, the African goddess of rivers and water. At midnight her followers flock to the beach to launch gifts on tiny boats. Tradition says that the goddess will not accept the gifts of those without virtue, so their boats will wash back to shore. To prevent this from happening, believers wade as far out from the beach as possible before releasing their offerings.

The same ceremony takes place in Salvador on February 2. On New Year's Day, Salvador joins other northeastern towns in celebrating the feast of the Lord Jesus of the Navigators. A parade of colorfully decorated ships escorts a statue of Jesus Christ across the harbor, as sailors believe that their homage to the Lord will protect them from harm.

INTERNET LINKS

www.rio-carnival.net/

The Rio Carnival website provides information and answers frequently asked questions about Carnival in Rio de Janeiro.

http://gobrazil.about.com/od/festivalsevents/Festivals_Events_ Special_Holidays_in_Brazil.htm

This website provides information about the major festivals in Brazil, including Carnival, Christmas, Easter, and other religious and nonreligious festivals.

www.braziltravelinformation.com/brazil_trip_planning_holidays_ listing.htm

This Brazil travel information website provides a calendar listing of the major Brazilian holidays and events that visitors should take note of before making travel plans. There are also links to additional information about some of the more popular holidays.

FOOD

A buffet spread shows the wide range of Brazilian cuisine.

13

BRAZIL'S CUISINE MIRRORS ITS culture. Brazilians use methods and ingredients introduced by European immigrants and African slaves in the past and by indigenous Indians past and present. As with other elements of Brazilian culture, the degree of influence of each contributor varies according to region.

The two staples of the Brazilian diet are manioc flour and beans. Manioc comes from the cassava plant. Indians on the northeastern coast cultivated this plant when the Portuguese first arrived in Brazil.

The Portuguese brought beans with them, as well as rice, sugarcane, and coffee. Traders on their way back from the Far East delivered cloves, cinnamon, and other spices. African slaves introduced bananas and a type of palm oil called *dendê* (dehn-DAY). *Dendê* oil remains a key ingredient in the typical dishes of the northeast.

FEIJOADA

Despite regional differences, there is one dish that brings the country together. Preparing and eating *feijoada* (fay-jhoo-AH-dah) is a weekly ritual in many restaurants and homes. The classic *feijoada* served in Rio de Janeiro combines black beans and various types of dried and smoked meats. This meal has developed with help from all three of Brazil's ethnic roots. Along with rice, a fried manioc-flour dish called *farofa* (fah-ROH-fah) is the main complement of the *feijoada*.

Many Brazilians enjoy eating out in self-service buffet-style restaurants called *comidas à quilo*, where food is paid for according to its weight.

The original *feijoada* recipe came from African slaves. In colonial days, the master kept the best cuts of meat for his family, giving his slaves the unwanted parts like the feet of the pig or the tongue of the cow. The slaves threw these leftovers into a pot with their beans, added onions, garlic, and a few other spices, and created a dish that eventually caught the master's attention.

Today many restaurants in Brazil serve two types of *feijoada*: *Feijoada tipica* (TEE-pih-kah) contains the traditional ingredients, including the eyes, ears, tongue, and tail of the animal; *feijoada moderna* (moh-DEHR-nah) sticks to more-conventional cuts, such as pork loin and beef brisket. Prepared either way, the end result is a delicious meal over which Brazilians can linger for two to three hours.

People warm up with a *caiprinha* (kah-ee-pee-REEN-yah), an alcoholic drink made with lime, sugar, and *cachaça* (kah-SHAH-sah), which is a liquor distilled from sugarcane. Then the main meal follows: a helping or two of beans, meat, rice, *farofa*, fresh oranges, and fried chopped kale.

BAHIAN FOOD

Bahia is home to Brazil's most distinctive cuisine. In this state, Portuguese and African styles of cooking combined with seafood and the tropical food of the northeastern coast produce a unique cuisine. Its ingredients are usually mashed and mixed in one pot and served over rice, manioc, or cornmeal. The rich taste of the ingredients, including *dendê* oil, coconut milk, dried shrimp or fish, crabmeat, and cashew nuts, soon wins over those who try it. The piquant taste of *malagueta* (mah-lah-GAY-tah) chili peppers balances the richness of these flavors. For those who like their food extra spicy, a bowl of pepper usually accompanies a Bahian dish.

Baianas are considered Brazil's best bakers of sweet food, though they are also famous for their main dishes. Dressed in white, *baianas* sell their specialties along the streets of cities like Salvador. Local favorites include *moqueca* (moh-EH-kah), *vatapá* (vah-tah-PAH), *caruru* (kah-ROO-roo), and *acarajé* (ah-kah-rah-JEH). *Moqueca* is a stew made with *dendê* oil, coconut milk, and fish or shrimp and spiced by *malagueta* peppers, garlic, and cloves. *Vatapá* is also a stew with ingredients similar to those in *moqueca*, except that it is thicker because manioc flour is added, and it tastes a little different

PAPOS DE ANJO (ANGEL'S CHEEKS)

These are sweet babas, or small yeast cakes. Called "angel's cheeks," they may have been invented by nuns.

2 egg whites
6 egg yolks
1 teaspoon (5 ml) yeast
1 teaspoon (5 ml) flour
¼ cup (60 ml) butter
2 ½ cups (625 ml) superfine sugar
2 cups (500 ml) water
1 teaspoon (5 ml) vanilla extract

Beat the egg whites until stiff. Add the egg yolks one at a time, beating continuously. Add the yeast and flour. Beat until a thick cream forms. Grease 20 small muffin tins with the butter. Fill them ¾ high with the mixture. Place tins in the oven at 400°F (205°C), and bake for 20 minutes. Remove the baked cakes from the tins, and arrange them on a shallow tray. Mix the sugar, water, and vanilla extract, and bring the mixture to a boil to make a syrup. Pour the syrup over the cakes, allowing the syrup to soak into them. Turn the cakes over so that they are evenly soaked.

because ginger is used in place of cloves. *Caruru* is a dish of shrimp and okra boiled in water, spiced with onions and peppers, and then mixed with *dendê* oil. *Acarajé* is a Brazilian fast food, the rough equivalent of the American hamburger. It is made from soaked and skinned local *fradinho* (frah-JIN-uh) beans, which are mashed together, mixed with diced shrimp and onions, and then fried in *dendê* oil.

PREPARING MANIOC FLOUR

Farmers in the north and the northeast still prepare manioc flour from the roots of the cassava plant, using the same technique indigenous Indians have been using for 400 years, although modern farmers employ slightly more-advanced technologies.

After the roots of the cassava plant have been picked and peeled, they are chopped in a grinder called a *cevadeira* (say-vah-DAY-reh). Metal blades inside this grinder are spun by a turning wheel.

The roots of the cassava plant contain poisonous prussic acid. To extract this poison, farmers use a levered press to pound the chopped cassava. The liquid that runs off contains the acid, and a paste that is left behind is what is wanted. This paste is run through a sieve to separate the thicker part, called *crueira* (croo-EH-rah).

The thin paste is boiled in an open pot and stirred constantly until it has been roasted dry. This powder is manioc flour.

OTHER REGIONAL FOODS

Seafood is the favorite food in most of the north. *Sururu* (soo-roo-ROO), a clam stew prepared in oyster sauce, and stuffed crab are favorite dishes in the state of Pernambuco. *Pirão* (pee-RAH-oo), a porridge prepared with manioc and fish broth, often accompanies seafood.

A Xingu Indian woman grates manioc flour to make soup.

Fresh meat and fish can be hard to come by in the hot northeastern *sertão*. *Carne de sol* (KAH-neh deh SOH), or dried salted meat, has become a staple. After slaughtering a cow, ranchers rub salt into the meat and hang it on racks to dry in the sun and wind. Another favorite in the *sertão* is the *buchada* (boo-SHAH-dah), a dish made from goat's liver, heart, and tripe.

The influence of indigenous Indians is still strong in the north, as the names of many dishes reveal. Residents of the states of Pará and Amazonas often eat fresh *pirarucu* (pee-rah-roo-KOO) and *tucunaré* (too-koo-nah-REH) fish served with a manioc sauce called *tucupi* (too-koo-PEE). They also enjoy a number of fruits unique to the Amazon. In the south, *churrasco* (cher-ras-KOH), meat on a spit slowly grilled and basted with saltwater for flavor, is the most popular meal. Brazilians either cook *churrascos* at home or go to *churrascaria* (shoo-hahs-kah-REE-ah) restaurants, where they eat all they can for a fixed price.

FRUITS OF BRAZIL

The forests of Brazil are a treasure chest of exquisite fruits. Ice-cream shops in cities such as Belém in Pará advertise 99 exotic fruit flavors. However, a U.S. or European visitor would have a hard time identifying most of these flavors. Here are a few examples of the fruits of Brazil:

ACAI *is the fruit of a palm tree called the açaizeiro (ah-sah-ee-ZAY-roh). It is common in the states of Amazonas and Pará. The flesh is usually mixed with sugar and served in a gourd or used to make wine. Northerners insist that any visitor who drinks acai wine will visit the region again. It is also known for its powerful antioxidant properties. Some even believe the acai berry can help in weight loss.*

GRAVIOLA *(grah-vee-OH-lah) comes from the same family as the pineapple. It is an oval fruit weighing 1 to 2 pounds (0.5 to 0.9 kg). A white, creamy meat and fine dark seeds lie inside its pale green skin. It tastes like a cross between a banana and a pineapple.*

JABOTICABA *is a red or black berry that originally grew in the wild but is now cultivated in different parts of Brazil. Its sweet, white pulp is used to make pies, jellies, and wines.*

JACA *(JAAH-kah) is the jackfruit from Southeast Asia. Traders brought it to Brazil in the 18th century, and it thrives in the tropical climate. The fruit can weigh up to 40 pounds (18 kg), and its pulp tastes rather sour. Brazilians use the pulp to make sweets and jellies, and they eat the seeds roasted.*

GOIABA *(goh-YAH-bah), or guava, is a yellow, pear-shaped fruit grown all over Brazil. One of the favorite fruits in the country, it is believed to stimulate the appetite when eaten before a meal and to aid digestion when eaten afterward.*

JENIPAPO *(jeh-nih-PAH-poo) is a light-brown fruit about the size of an apple. It originated in the Antilles and thrives in Brazil's north, where Indians use its dark pulp to blacken their faces. When ripe, the jenipapo skin is thin and soft, and the watery pulp has a sweet-and-sour taste.*

FOOD CUSTOMS

Breakfast is usually a light meal for most Brazilians, with some fruit accompanying buttered bread and coffee. Lunch, generally the biggest meal of the day, regularly takes up to two hours. Many employers grant extended lunch breaks to allow workers to enjoy this meal at home. Dinner is served quite late, usually around 8:30 P.M. In between lunch and dinner, many people have a *lanche* (LAHN-cheh), a light snack with coffee or juice.

Brazilians consider good table manners to be a sign of a good education and hence of good social standing. Those with good manners do not use bare hands to pick up food. They use a fork and knife for everything, including apples, oranges, sandwiches, chicken legs, and pizzas. A growing number of U.S.-style fast-food restaurants are gradually changing this traditional social rule, but many people continue to carefully wrap a napkin around their hamburgers.

Friends catching up over a cup of coffee at a café in São Paulo.

Children may eat an ice-cream cone while walking down the street, but Brazilians consider it rude for an adult to eat in public. Those who buy food from a streetside vendor usually eat it on the spot. This habit stems from the belief that food should be shared. Any time Brazilians are eating, be it a meal at home or a candy bar on the beach, they offer to share it with any friend who comes along.

When food is offered, it is considered rude to say no without offering a good excuse. Similarly, hosts are expected to provide more than enough food for their guests, and guests are expected to try their best to eat all of it.

DRINKS

Coffee is Brazil's national drink. A *cafezinho* (kah-feh-ZEEN-yoo) is a mandatory part of any social event, be it lunch with the family at home or a business meeting in the office. *Cafezinho* means "little coffee," and this very strong brew is served in a cup one-third the size of an American coffee cup.

Brazilians add lots of sugar to their *cafezinho* to counter the strength of the brew. Businesspeople in Brazil often start their meetings with *cafezinhos* all around. They have a friendly chat while drinking, and serious talk begins only when the cups are empty. The opposite occurs at mealtime; the *cafezinho* comes after the meal is finished.

Good drink and conversation are hallmarks of the sidewalk bars and cafés. Whether stopping by on the way home from the beach or meeting friends after dinner, Brazilians spend a lot of time in bars and cafés. They drink fruit juices, such as coconut milk or freshly squeezed mango, and fruit milkshakes.

Popular milkshakes use ingredients such as raw oatmeal, avocado, papaya, and banana. *Guarana* (goo-ah-rah-NAH), a unique Brazilian soft drink, is made from a small tropical fruit. Beer and *cachaça* are popular at night. Bartenders combine *cachaça* with different fruits to make drinks called *batidas* (bah-CHEE-dahs).

Wine is becoming increasingly popular. Almost all of Brazil's wine comes from Rio Grande do Sul, where vineyards started by Italian immigrants continue to improve the quality of Brazilian wine.

INTERNET LINKS

www.globalgourmet.com/destinations/brazil/#axzz1EVjxGU5A

This Global Gourmet website provides information on the history, influences, and customs of Brazil's interesting cuisine, including recipes and a menu guide.

www.foodbycountry.com/Algeria-to-France/Brazil.html

This website provides information about the history of food in Brazil, including types of food eaten at religious festivals.

www.cookbrazil.com/

This website provides easy-to-make Brazilian recipes, such as *feijoada* and *caipirinha*, adapted for the American kitchen.

FEIJOADA (MEAT AND BLACK BEAN STEW)

This is Brazil's national dish. *Feijoa* means "black beans" in Portuguese. This recipe serves five people.

1 pound (450 g) black beans

10 cups (2.5 L) water

2 cups (500 ml) beef stock

1 pound (450 g) smoked sausage

$\frac{1}{2}$ pound (225 g) bacon

4 pork shoulder bones and ears

3 tablespoons (45 ml) olive oil

2 small onions

2 garlic cloves

2 large bay leaves

Salt and fresh pepper

Hot pepper sauce

Wash the black beans well and soak in four cups (1 L) of water overnight. Add beef stock and cook for an hour over low heat, stirring occasionally to avoid burning. Cut sausage, bacon, and pork into bite-size pieces and place in a pan. Cover with five cups (1.2 l) of water and boil for 10 minutes, then carefully drain away the water. Heat olive oil in a pan, and fry onions and garlic to form a caramel. Add some of the cooked beans to the fried onions and garlic, and mash. Add bay leaves and fry for a few minutes. Pour mixture into the rest of the cooked beans. Add the strained meats and one cup (235 ml) water. Stir, then add salt, pepper, and hot pepper sauce to taste. When the liquid is thick and flavorful, serve over rice and garnish with orange slices.

RABANADAS (PORTUGUESE FRIED TOAST)

This recipe serves four to six people.

8 slices white bread

2 cups (500 ml) milk

1 cup plus 2 tablespoons (280 ml) sugar

1 tablespoon (15 ml) ground cinnamon

Pinch of salt

3 large eggs, separated

1 cup (250 ml) vegetable oil

Heat oven between 140ºF and 175ºF (60ºC and 80ºC). Cut bread in half diagonally, or use a cookie cutter to cut out circles. Put milk and two tablespoons of sugar in a large, shallow bowl and stir. Leave bread to soak in the milk-and-sugar mixture for 10 minutes. Mix cinnamon, salt, and the rest of the sugar together in a bowl. Set aside. Put egg whites in a clean bowl. Using an electric mixer, beat until egg whites are thick and stand in stiff peaks when the beaters are lifted. Add egg yolks and beat again until thick. Heat a few tablespoons of oil in a large skillet over medium heat. Remove bread from milk, slice by slice, and dip in eggs. Add to skillet and fry until golden. Using a spatula, turn over. Continue frying until golden. Drain on paper towels. Put on a plate, and sprinkle with cinnamon sugar. Keep warm in oven.

MAP OF BRAZIL

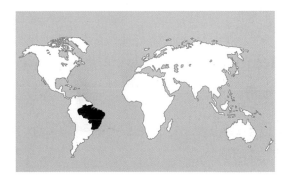

ECONOMIC BRAZIL

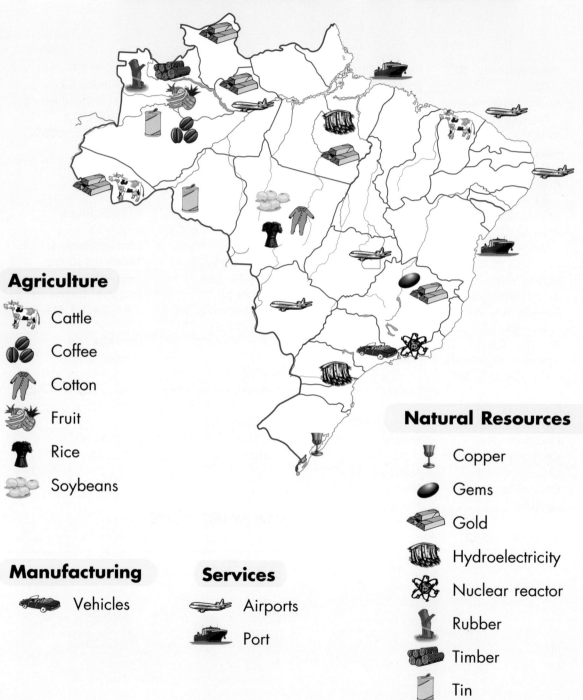

Agriculture

- Cattle
- Coffee
- Cotton
- Fruit
- Rice
- Soybeans

Manufacturing

- Vehicles

Services

- Airports
- Port

Natural Resources

- Copper
- Gems
- Gold
- Hydroelectricity
- Nuclear reactor
- Rubber
- Timber
- Tin

ABOUT THE ECONOMY

OVERVIEW

Brazil is the largest economy in South America and one of the world's top five economies. Although Brazil suffered the effects of the global financial crisis in 2008, it has made a strong recovery. In 2010 its growth rate stood at 7.5 percent compared with 5.1 percent in 2008. Previously Brazil's growth had been curtailed by huge foreign debt, but since 2003 it reduced its debt so effectively that by 2008, Brazil became a net external creditor. In 2011 it wished to limit inflation and promote economic growth and was using a wide variety of economic techniques in order to achieve these goals.

GROSS DOMESTIC PRODUCT (GDP)

$2.024 trillion (2010 estimate)

GDP PER CAPITA

$10,900 (2010 estimate)

GDP COMPOSITION

Agriculture: 6.1 percent
Industry: 26.4 percent
Services: 67.5 percent (2010 estimate)

CURRENCY

Real (R) = 100 centavos
US$1 = R$1.61 (2011 estimate)

GDP GROWTH

7.5 percent (2010 estimate)

EXTERNAL DEBT

41 percent of GDP (2011 estimate)

INFLATION RATE

6.5 percent (2011 estimate)

AGRICULTURAL PRODUCTS

Coffee, soybeans, wheat, rice, corn, cocoa, citrus, sugarcane, beef

MAIN EXPORTS

Transportation equipment, soybeans, iron ore, footwear, coffee, autos

MAIN EXPORT PARTNERS

European Union 24.12 percent, China 13.49 percent, United States 11.33 percent, Argentina 8.98 percent, Japan 3.08 percent (2009 estimate)

MAIN IMPORTS

Machinery, electrical and transportation equipment, chemical products, refined oil, automotive parts, electronics

MAIN IMPORT PARTNERS

United States 16 percent, China 13 percent, Argentina 9 percent, Germany 8 percent, Japan 4 percent (2009 estimate)

LABOR FORCE

103.6 million (2010 estimate)

UNEMPLOYMENT RATE

6.5 percent (2011 estimate)

CULTURAL BRAZIL

Amazonian Rain Forest
The lungs of the earth, this forest is home to many unique species of plants and animals, some of which are in danger of extinction, while others have yet to be discovered.

Feast of Our Lady of Nazareth
Some 2 million people participate in Cirio, a procession of faith in honor of Our Lady of Nazareth.

Colonial architecture
Famous for its beautiful colonial architecture, the city of São Luís boasts many magnificent churches and gorgeous palaces.

Folklore Festival
Characters from Brazilian folklore come to life through skits, music, and the clothing of *maracatu* and *chula* dancers.

Old capital city
Located on the Bay of All Saints, Salvador is Brazil's former colonial capital city. Once the slave center of Brazil, this old city is beautiful as well as quaint with its narrow cobblestone streets. Highlights include Farol da Barra, a 16th-century fortified lighthouse, and 17th-century antiques at the Museu de Arte da Bahia and Museu de Arte Sac

Manaus Opera House
Also known as the Amazon Theater. Has a golden dome covered with 36,000 ceramic tiles, a ceiling painted with scenes of music, dance, and drama.

Carnival
Crowds throng the streets of Maceió in a celebration of indulgences before 40 days of fasting and abstinence leading up to Easter.

Masquerades
Dancers, drummers, and singers dressed in elaborate costumes lead a massive, nightlong street party filled with music, food, and alcohol.

Pelourinho
Within the older part of the upper city of Salvador is a city within a city, known as Pelourinho. Pelourinho is a UNESCO World Heritage Site and of national historic importance, as it was where slave auctions took place before slavery was outlawed in 1835.

Iguaçú Falls
Some 275 waterfalls spread over a two-mile (3.2-km) area. The most spectacular point is at Devil's Throat, where 14 falls curve around a 369-foot (82-m) drop.

Basílica do Senhor Bom Jesus de Matosinhos
Chapels here contain 64 life-sized statues dramatizing the scenes of the Passion of Jesus Christ and 12 soapstone statues of Old Testament prophets.

Oktoberfest
The second-largest festival in Brazil and second-largest beer festival in the world displays typical German dances and costumes to revive the customs and culture of German immigrants who came to Brazil.

Cristo Redentor
From the top of Corcovado (Hunchback) Mountain, a concrete statue of Christ the Redeemer—at a height of 125 feet (38 m) and spanning 92 feet (28 m) across the arms—towers over Rio de Janeiro.

Copacabana and Ipanema
World-famous beaches, one of the loveliest bays in the world, and a wonderful climate blending summer and spring make Rio a true sun, sand, and sea city.

ETHNIC GROUPS
White 48.2 percent, mulatto (mixed white and black) 44.2 percent, black 6.9 percent, others (includes Japanese, Arab, Amerindian) 0.7 percent (2010 estimate)

MAIN RELIGIONS
Roman Catholic 73.6 percent, Protestant 15.4 percent, Spiritualist 1.3 percent, Bantu/voodoo 0.3 percent, other 1.8 percent, unspecified 0.2 percent, none 7.4 percent (2000 estimate)

OFFICIAL NAME
Federative Republic of Brazil

FLAG DESCRIPTION
Green background with a large yellow diamond in the center bearing a blue celestial globe with 27 white five-point stars arranged in the pattern of the night sky. The globe has a white equatorial band with the motto *Ordem e Progresso* (Order and Progress).

MAJOR LANGUAGES
Portuguese (the official and most widely spoken language); less common languages include Spanish (border areas and schools), German, Italian, Japanese, English, and numerous minor Amerindian languages

LITERACY
88.6 percent of population aged 15 and above

POPULATION
203,429,773 (2010 estimate)

LIFE EXPECTANCY
Total population 72.53 years
Male 68.97 years; female 76.27 years (2010 estimate)

ADMINISTRATIVE DIVISIONS
26 states (*estados*) and 1 federal district (*distrito federal*)

AGE STRUCTURE
0—14 years: 26.7 percent of population
15—64 years: 66.8 percent
65 years and above: 6.4 percent (2011 estimate)

NATIONAL HOLIDAY
New Year's Day (January 1), Carnival (February/March), Easter (March/April), Tiradentes Day (April 21), Labor Day (May 1), Corpus Christi (May/June), Independence Day (September 7), Nossa Senhora de Aparecida Day (October 12), All Souls' Day (November 2), Proclamation of the Republic (November 15), Christmas (December 25)

TIME LINE

IN BRAZIL	IN THE WORLD
1494	
Treaty of Tordesillas divides the New World between Spain and Portugal, giving the as-yet-undiscovered area of Brazil to Portugal.	
1530	**1530**
Coastal Brazil is distributed to Portuguese captains for growing sugarcane.	Beginning of transatlantic slave trade organized by Portuguese in Africa
1565	**1558–1603**
Rio de Janeiro is founded.	Reign of Elizabeth I of England
1654	
The Dutch are expelled from Brazil.	
1693	
Era of gold and diamond mining begins.	
1727	
Coffee is introduced into Brazil.	**1776**
1789	U.S. Declaration of Independence
First efforts to establish a republic are crushed.	
1807	
Napoleon invades Portugal. King João VI and his family flee to Brazil.	
1815	
Brazil is declared a kingdom.	
1822	
João VI's son Pedro declares Brazil's independence from Portugal and is crowned emperor of Brazil.	
1831	
Pedro I abdicates and leaves the throne to his five-year-old son, Pedro II.	
1841	
Pedro II is crowned emperor at the age of 14.	**1861**
1864–70	U.S. Civil War begins.
War of the Triple Alliance—Argentina, Brazil, and Uruguay fight Paraguay.	
1888	
The Golden Law abolishes the practice of owning slaves.	
1889	
The army deposes Pedro II and proclaims a republic.	
1891	
The first Brazilian Constitution is created.	

IN BRAZIL	IN THE WORLD
1894 Brazil's first civilian president, José de Morais Barros, takes office	
	1914 World War I begins.
1932 São Paulo rebellion results in civil war.	
1934 New constitution is adopted; Getúlio Vargas is elected to the presidency.	
1937 Estado Novo, or "New State," is established.	**1939** World War II begins.
1964 A military coup puts Marshal Humberto de Alencar Castelo Branco in power.	**1966–1969** Chinese Cultural Revolution
1985 The military steps down; democracy is restored.	**1986** Nuclear power disaster at Chernobyl in Ukraine
1988 A new constitution goes into effect.	
1989 The first direct presidential election since 1960 is held.	**1991** Breakup of Soviet Union
1994 The constitution is revised to reduce the presidential term to four years; Fernando Henrique Cardoso is elected for the first time.	**1997** Hong Kong is returned to China.
1998 Cardoso is reelected for a second term. IMF provides rescue package after economy is hit by collapse of Asian stock markets.	
2001 Government commits to spend $40 billion to develop the Amazon Basin.	**2001** World population surpasses 6 billion.
2002 Brazil celebrates its fifth FIFA World Cup victory. Lula da Silva wins presidential elections and pledges to eradicate hunger.	**2003** War in Iraq begins.
2006 President Lula is reelected.	**2009** Outbreak of flu virus H1N1 around the world
2010 Dilma Rousseff of the Workers' Party wins second-round presidential runoff.	
2011 The historic inauguration of Brazil's first female president, Dilma Rousseff.	**2011** Twin earthquake and tsunami disasters strike northeast Japan, leaving over 14,000 dead.

GLOSSARY

abraço (ah-BRAH-soo)
Hug used as a greeting among men.

baiana (bah-YAH-nah)
Woman from the northern state of Bahia.

bandeirante (bahn-day-RAHN-teh)
Early frontiersman of Brazil's interior regions.

beijinhos (bay-JIN-hoos)
A form of greeting where women kiss other women on the cheek two or three times.

caboclo (kah-BOH-cloh)
Brazilian of European and Indian ancestry.

cafuso (kah-FOO-soh)
Brazilian of African and Indian ancestry.

candomblé (kahn-dohm-BLEH)
African religion whose adherents believe in the possession of human participants by supernatural spirits.

churrasco (shoo-HAHS-koo)
Meat roasted on a spit, a popular dish in the south of Brazil.

à quilo (kom-ee-dah-A-kee-loh)
Simple and inexpensive restaurant where food is paid for by weight.

dendê (dehn-DAY)
Palm oil used in cooking.

favela
Slum in Brazilian cities.

frevo (FRAY-voh)
Music and dance style of northeast Brazil.

futebol or *futbol* (FOOT-ball)
Soccer, the most popular game in Brazil.

jeito (JAY-toh)
"A way"—slang term referring to a knack for completing difficult tasks.

macumba
African religion in which it is believed that the living can communicate with the souls of the dead.

moreno (mo-RAY-noh) or mulatto
Brazilian of European and African ancestry; nowadays *moreno* and *Afrodescente* are more commonly used than "mulatto."

orixás (oh-ree-SHAHS)
African gods brought to Brazil by the slaves.

telenovelas
Long-running serials aired during prime time in Brazil.

FOR FURTHER INFORMATION

BOOKS

Brainard, Lael. *Brazil As an Economic Superpower? Understanding Brazil's Changing Role in the Global Economy.* Washington, D.C.: Brookings Institution Press, 2009.

De Carvalho, Sarah. *The Street Children of Brazil: One Woman's Remarkable Story.* London: Hodder & Stoughton, 2009.

Marshall, Oliver, et al. *The Rough Guide to Brazil.* London: Rough Guides, 2009.

Parker, Ed. *Brazil* (Discover Countries). London: Wayland, 2010.

Platt, Richard. *The Vanishing Rainforest.* London: Frances Lincoln, 2007.

Robinson, Alex. *Brazil Handbook Footprint Travel Guides.* London: Footprint Travel Guides, 2009.

Robinson, Alex. *DK Eyewitness Travel Guide: Brazil.* London: Dorling Kindersley, 2010.

Roett, Riordan. *The New Brazil.* Washington, D.C.: Brookings Institution, 2010.

Rohter, Larry. *Brazil on the Rise: The Story of a Country Transformed.* Basingstoke, England: Palgrave Macmillan, 2010.

St. Louis, Regis. *Brazil* (Lonely Planet Country Guides). London: Lonely Planet Publications, 2010.

FILMS/DVDS

Brazil: An Inconvenient History. Seventh Arts, 2008.

Brazil, Giant of the South. TravelVideoStore.com, 2008.

Brazil—Rio de Janiero. Wild Life International, 2010.

The Boys from Brazil: The Official History of the Brazilian World Cup Team 1930 to 1986. Entertain Video, 2006.

Capoeira, Brazil's Secret Fighting Art. Yamazato Videos, 2003.

Central Station. Walt Disney Studios Home Entertainment, 2004.

City of God (Cidade De Deus). Walt Disney Studios Home Entertainment, 2003.

Discovery Atlas: Brazil Revealed. Discovery Channel, 2007.

Families of Brazil. Big Kids Productions, 2010.

Globe Trekker: Destination Brazil. Pilot Productions, 2002.

Pilot Guides—Destination Brazil. Pilot Productions, 2002.

Ronaldo—A Legend in the Making. 4digital Media, 2004.

Samba—Popular Music of Brazil. Fremeaux, 2005.

BIBLIOGRAPHY

BOOKS

Harrison, Phyllis. *Behaving Brazilian: A Comparison of Brazilian and North American Social Behavior.* Rowley, MA: Newbury House Publishers, 1983.

Taylor, Edwin, ed. *Insight Guides: Brazil.* Singapore: APA Publications, 1989.

Mortality in Brazil, 1950-2000: Social Progress and Persistent Racial Inequality. Latin American Research Review, Vol. 45, No. 2, 2010, pp. 114—139.

WEBSITES

BBC News: Brazil Country Profile, www.bbc.co.uk/2/hi/europe/country_profiles/1227110.stm

Birds of the Pantanal, www.pantanalbirds.com/

Brazil Climate, www.climatetemp.info/brazil/

Brazil Council, www.brazilcouncil.org/information-brazil/policy-trade-economy

Brazil Link, www.brazilink.org/Brazil%2C+rural%2C+government&highlight=ministerio

Brazil: Main Economic Indicators, http://trade.ec.europa.eu/doclib/docs/2006/september/tradoc_113359.pdf

CIA World Fact Book: Brazil, www.cia.gov/library/publications/the-world-factbook/geos/br.html

EconomyWatch: Brazil's Trade, Export and Import, www.economywatch.com/world_economy/brazil/export-import.html

Greenpeace: Brazil. www.greenpeace.org.br/

EFA 2000 Assessment: Country Reports—Brazil, www.unesco.org/education/wef/countryreports/brazil/rapport_2.html

Encyclopedia of the Nations: Brazil, www.nationsencyclopedia.com/Americas/Brazil.html

Fact Monster: Brazil, www.factmonster.com/ce6/world/A0857011.html

Federative Republic of Brazil, www.brasil.gov.br/brazil/home-en/contentpanels_view?set_language=en

FinanceAsia: The Growing Importance of China-Brazil Trade, www.financeasia.com/News/239307,the-growing-importance-of-china-brazil-trade.aspx

Library of Congress Country Studies: Brazil, http://lcweb2.loc.gov/frd/cs/brtoc.html

UNICEF, www.unicef.org/infobycountry/brazil_statistics.html

United Nations High Commissioner for Refugees (UNHCR) Country Profiles: Brazil., www.unhcr.ch/world/amer/brazil.htm

VivaBrazil, www.vivabrazil.com

INDEX

INDEX